Math in Focus®
Singapore Math
by Marshall Cavendish

Activity Book

Author

Ang Kok Cheng

Marshall Cavendish
Education

US Distributor

COMMON
CORE

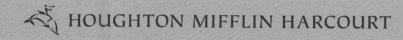

HOUGHTON MIFFLIN HARCOURT

© 2012 Marshall Cavendish International (Singapore) Private Limited

Published by Marshall Cavendish Education
An imprint of Marshall Cavendish International (Singapore) Private Limited
Times Centre, 1 New Industrial Road, Singapore 536196
Customer Service Hotline: (65) 6411 0820
E-mail: tmesales@sg.marshallcavendish.com
Website: www.marshallcavendish.com/education

Distributed by
Houghton Mifflin Harcourt
222 Berkeley Street
Boston, MA 02116
Tel: 617-351-5000
Website: www.hmheducation.com/mathinfocus

Common Core State Standards © Copyright 2010.
National Governors Association Center for Best Practices and
Council of Chief State School Officers. All rights reserved.

This product is not sponsored or endorsed by the Common Core State Standards
Initiative of the National Governors Association Center for Best Practices and
the Council of Chief State School Officers.

First published 2012
Reprinted 2012 (twice)

Math in Focus® Activity Book Course 1
ISBN 978-0-547-57897-2

Printed in Singapore

3 4 5 6 7 8   1401   16 15 14 13 12
4500346056   A B C D E

Contents

Math in Focus®

Singapore Math
by Marshall Cavendish

Introducing Math in Focus® Activity Book

The *Activity Book*, created to complement *Math in Focus®*: **Singapore Math by Marshall Cavendish**, provides additional projects and activities to deepen students' mathematical experiences. These projects and activities allow students to model mathematics, reason abstractly about new content, make sense of non-routine problems, and persevere in solving them.

Using the Activity Book

The *Activity Book* contains either a paper-and-pencil activity or a technology activity to accompany one lesson in each chapter of *Math in Focus*. It also contains a project for each chapter that can be done either with a partner or a small group. Some activities and projects can be used as an alternate approach to what is taught in the Student Book, and others are extensions of what is in the Student Book. Each activity and project includes a scoring rubric, recording sheets and templates for students, and an answer key with solutions.

The *Activity Book* is also available online and on the Teacher One Stop CD-ROM.

Positive Numbers and the Number Line

Lesson 1.2 Activity: A Property of Prime Numbers

Teacher's Guide

Type of activity	Hands-on activity
Objective	Reinforce the skill of identifying prime numbers.
Material	Calculator
Time	20–30 min
Ability levels	Mixed
Prerequisite skills	Find the sum, product, and quotient of whole numbers.
Grouping	Students should work with a partner or in a small group.
Assessment of students' learning	See Lesson 1.2 Activity: Rubric.

Lesson 1.2 Activity Rubric

Category	4	3	2	1
Mathematical concepts	Explanation shows complete understanding of the mathematical concepts used to solve the problem(s).	Explanation shows substantial understanding of the mathematical concepts used to solve the problem(s).	Explanation shows some understanding of the mathematical concepts needed to solve the problem(s).	Explanation shows very limited understanding of the underlying concepts needed to solve the problem(s) OR is not written.
Reflection	The reflection shows tremendous thought and effort. The learning experience being reflected upon is relevant and meaningful to student and learning goals.	The reflection shows a lot of thought and effort. Student makes attempts to demonstrate relevance, but the relevance is unclear in reference to learning goals.	The reflection shows some thought and effort. Some sections of the reflection is irrelevant to student and/or learning goals.	The reflection is superficial. Most of the reflection is irrelevant to student and/or learning goals.

Lesson 1.2 Activity
A Property of Prime Numbers

Step 1 Choose any prime number greater than 5.

Step 2 Find the square of the number.

Step 3 Add 17 to the result of Step 2.

Step 4 Divide the result of Step 3 by 12. What is the remainder?

Step 5 Record your result in the table on the Student Recording Sheet.

Step 6 Repeat Steps 1–5 ten times, starting with a different prime number each time.

Step 7 What do you notice about the result?

Lesson 1.2 Activity
Student Recording Sheet

Prime number										
Square of the prime number										
Add 17										
Divide by 12										
Remainder										

1. What do you notice about the table?

2. What conclusion can you draw from your results?

Reflection

3. How can you use this conclusion in working with prime numbers?

CHAPTER 1   Positive Numbers and the Number Line

Project: Expressing a Square as the Sum of Two Prime Numbers

Teacher's Guide

Common Core State Standard	6.EE.1 Write and evaluate numerical expressions involving whole-number exponents.
Objective	Reinforce the skill of evaluating exponential expressions by writing perfect squares as sums of two prime numbers.
Material	Calculator
Time	15–20 min
Ability levels	Mixed
Prerequisite skills	Identify prime numbers less than 225. Find the square of a whole number.
Grouping	Students should work with a partner or in a small group.
Assessment of students' learning	See Chapter 1 Project: Rubric.
Preparation	If students have difficulty beginning the project, suggest that they list all the squares of numbers from 5 to 15, then list all the prime numbers up to 225, the square of 15. *Extension:* The project may be extended to squares of numbers greater than 15.

Chapter 1 Project
Rubric

Category	4	3	2	1
Mathematical concepts	Explanation shows complete understanding of the mathematical concepts used to solve the problem(s).	Explanation shows substantial understanding of the mathematical concepts used to solve the problem(s).	Explanation shows some understanding of the mathematical concepts needed to solve the problem(s).	Explanation shows very limited understanding of the underlying concepts needed to solve the problem(s) OR is not written.
Mathematical reasoning	Uses complex and refined mathematical reasoning.	Uses effective mathematical reasoning.	Shows some evidence of mathematical reasoning.	Shows little evidence of mathematical reasoning.
Strategy/ Procedures	Uses an efficient and effective strategy to solve the problem(s).	Uses an effective strategy to solve the problem(s).	Uses an effective strategy to solve the problem(s), but does not do it consistently.	Does not use an effective strategy to solve the problem(s).
Working with others	Student was an engaged partner, listening to suggestions of others and working cooperatively throughout the lesson.	Student was an engaged partner but had trouble listening to others and/or working cooperatively.	Student cooperated with others, but needed prompting to stay on task.	Student did not work effectively with others.

Chapter 1 Project
Expressing a Square as the Sum of Two Prime Numbers

1. In this project, you will explore whether the square of every whole number from 5 to 15 can be written as the sum of two prime numbers. An example is shown in the table.

Number	Square	Square written as the sum of two prime numbers
4	$4^2 = 16$	16 = 3 + 13 or 16 = 5 + 11

2. As you work, think about these questions:

   - Is the square of an even number *odd* or *even*?
   - Is the square of an odd number *odd* or *even*?
   - Is the sum of two even numbers *even* or *odd*?
   - Is the sum of two odd numbers *even* or *odd*?
   - What type of numbers do you add to make an odd number?
   - Can the square of every number be written as the sum of two prime numbers?

3. Answer the questions on the Student Recording Sheet, and write a brief summary of your results. Include the sum you found for each square and the answers to the questions on the Student Recording Sheet.

Chapter 1 Project
Student Recording Sheet

1. Write each square as the sum of two prime numbers, if possible.
   Show all your work.

2. Which squares are even numbers? Which are odd numbers?

3. What type of numbers must you add to make an even number? What type
   of numbers must you add to make an odd number?

4. Can every square from 5 to 15 be written as the sum of two prime numbers?
   Why or why not? Explain, based on your answers to Questions 2 and 3.

Negative Numbers and the Number Line

Lesson 2.1 Activity: Negative Numbers

Teacher's Guide

Type of activity	Hands-on activity/game
Objective	Reinforce the skill of representing, comparing, and ordering positive and negative numbers on the number line.
Materials	• Number cube, numbered 1 to 6 • Sheet of paper with the number line drawn on it • Marker or counter
Time	20–30 min
Ability levels	Mixed
Prerequisite skills	Represent positive and negative numbers on the number line.
Grouping	Students should work with a partner or in a small group.
Assessment of students' learning	See Lesson 2.1 Activity: Rubric.

Lesson 2.1 Activity
Rubric

Category	4	3	2	1
Mathematical concepts	Explanation shows complete understanding of the mathematical concepts used to solve the problem(s).	Explanation shows substantial understanding of the mathematical concepts used to solve the problem(s).	Explanation shows some understanding of the mathematical concepts needed to solve the problem(s).	Explanation shows very limited understanding of the underlying concepts needed to solve the problem(s) OR is not written.
Reflection	The reflection shows tremendous thought and effort. The learning experience being reflected upon is relevant and meaningful to student and learning goals.	The reflection shows a lot of thought and effort. Student makes attempts to demonstrate relevance, but the relevance is unclear in reference to learning goals.	The reflection shows some thought and effort. Some sections of the reflection is irrelevant to student and/or learning goals.	The reflection is superficial. Most of the reflection is irrelevant to student and/or learning goals.

Lesson 2.1 Activity
Negative Numbers

Tug o' Numbers

Materials:
- Number cube
- Marker or counter
- Number line

This game is played by two players.

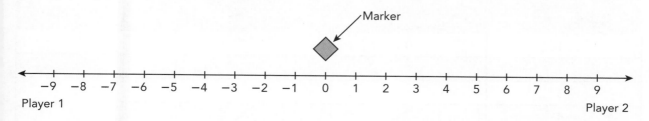

Step 1 Player 1 uses the negative side of the number line and Player 2 uses the positive side. Place the marker above 0 on the number line.

Step 2 Player 1 tosses the number cube. Player 1 moves the marker to the left according to the number shown on the cube. For example, if Player 1 gets a 4, the marker is moved 4 units to the left, above −4.

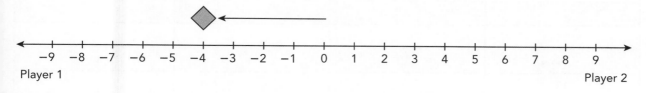

Step 3 Player 2 tosses the number cube. Player 2 moves the marker to the right according to the number shown on the cube, starting from its last position. For example, if Player 2 gets a 6, the marker is moved 6 places to the right, above 2.

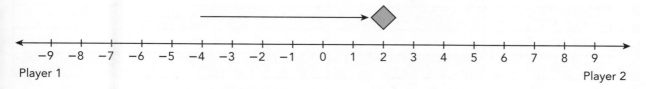

Step 4 The game ends after 10 turns for each player. The player on whose side the marker ends wins the game.

Lesson 2.1 Activity
Student Recording Sheet

Example

Turn	Position of the marker	Tug	New position of the marker
1	0	4	−4
2	−4	6	2

Turn	Position of the marker	Tug	New position of the marker
1	0		
2			
3			
4			
5			
6			
7			
8			
9			
10			
11			
12			
13			
14			
15			
16			
17			
18			
19			
20			

Note: The unshaded rows are for Player 1. The shaded rows are for Player 2.

Reflection

What did you learn from this activity?

CHAPTER 2   Negative Numbers and the Number Line

Project: Opposites on a Number Line

Teacher's Guide

Common Core	
Common Core State Standard	6.NS.6a Recognize that the opposite of the opposite of a number is the number itself . . . .
Objective	Order and compare negative numbers by representing them on a number line.
Materials	• Two different-colored pencils or pens • Calculator (optional)
Time	20–30 min
Ability levels	Advanced
Prerequisite skills	Identify the opposite of a number. Graph numbers on a number line.
Grouping	Students should work with a partner or in a small group.
Assessment of students' learning	See Chapter 2 Project: Rubric.

Chapter 2 Project
Rubric

Category	4	3	2	1
Mathematical concepts	Explanation shows complete understanding of the mathematical concepts used to solve the problem(s).	Explanation shows substantial understanding of the mathematical concepts used to solve the problem(s).	Explanation shows some understanding of the mathematical concepts needed to solve the problem(s).	Explanation shows very limited understanding of the underlying concepts needed to solve the problem(s) OR is not written.
Mathematical reasoning	Uses complex and refined mathematical reasoning.	Uses effective mathematical reasoning.	Shows some evidence of mathematical reasoning.	Shows little evidence of mathematical reasoning.
Strategy/ Procedures	Typically uses an efficient and effective strategy to solve the problem(s).	Typically uses an effective strategy to solve the problem(s).	Sometimes uses an effective strategy to solve the problem(s), but does not do it consistently.	Rarely uses an effective strategy to solve the problem(s).
Working with others	Student was an engaged partner, listening to suggestions of others and working cooperatively throughout the lesson.	Student was an engaged partner but had trouble listening to others and/or working cooperatively.	Student cooperated with others, but needed prompting to stay on task.	Student did not work effectively with others.

Chapter 2 Project
Opposites on a Number Line

1. On the Student Recording Sheet, choose an appropriate scale and graph the numbers 8, −3, 5, 4, 0, 2, −5, and −1 on the number line.

2. On the Student Recording Sheet, choose an appropriate scale and graph the numbers 2, 2.5, 0.25, 0, −2.5, 2, −0.75, and −1.5 on the number line.

3. On the Student Recording Sheet, choose an appropriate scale and graph the numbers 150, 0, −125, 125, −200, 250, and −100 on the number line.

4. Using a different-colored pen or pencil, graph the opposite of each number that you graphed in Steps 1–3 on the same number line. Remember that the opposite of 0 is itself.

5. Answer the questions on the Student Recording Sheet.

Chapter 2 Project
Student Recording Sheet

1. ←——————————————————————————→

2. ←——————————————————————————→

3. ←——————————————————————————→

Answer these questions.

4. When you graphed the opposites of the numbers, what did you notice?

5. What is the opposite of a number n? What is the opposite of $-n$?

6. Explain why the opposite of a negative number is positive.

Multiplying and Dividing Fractions and Decimals

Lesson 3.1 Activity: Computing with Fractions

Teacher's Guide

Type of activity	Hands-on activity/game
Objective	Reinforce the skill of performing operations with fractions, mixed numbers, and whole numbers.
Materials	Number and operation cards on pages 21–26: • 10 cards with whole numbers • 10 cards with fractions • 10 cards with mixed numbers • 20 operation cards (5 each for +, −, ×, and ÷)
Time	20–30 min
Ability levels	Mixed
Prerequisite skills	Solve problems involving addition, subtraction, multiplication, and division of fractions, whole numbers, and mixed numbers.
Grouping	Students should work with a partner.
Assessment of students' learning	See Lesson 3.1 Activity: Rubric.
Preparation	Rearrange the numbers if the problem shown by the cards will result in negative numbers. For example, instead of $\frac{1}{2} - \frac{5}{6}$, change the problem to $\frac{5}{6} - \frac{1}{2}$.

Lesson 3.1 Activity
Rubric

Category	4	3	2	1
Mathematical concepts	Explanation shows complete understanding of the mathematical concepts used to solve the problem(s).	Explanation shows substantial understanding of the mathematical concepts used to solve the problem(s).	Explanation shows some understanding of the mathematical concepts needed to solve the problem(s).	Explanation shows very limited understanding of the underlying concepts needed to solve the problem(s) OR is not written.
Self-assessment	Self-assessment is accurate and explanation is detailed and clear.	Self-assessment is fairly accurate and explanation is clear.	Self-assessment is inaccurate and explanation is a little difficult to understand, but includes critical components.	Self-assessment is totally inaccurate and explanation is difficult to understand and is missing several components OR is not included.

Lesson 3.1 Activity
Computing with Fractions

Step 1 Player 1 shuffles the stack of cards for whole numbers, fractions, and mixed numbers (Stack A).

Step 2 Player 2 shuffles the operation cards (Stack B).

Step 3 Player 1 draws two cards from Stack A and places them face down on a table.

Step 4 Player 2 draws 1 card from Stack B and places it face down between the two cards drawn by Player 1.

Step 5 At the count of three, all three cards are turned over. Players have 1 minute to solve the problem shown by the cards. All answers must be expressed in simplest form.

Players earn 2 points for every correct answer and 1 point for every answer that is correct, but not written in simplest form. 1 point is deducted for every wrong answer. No point is awarded for an answer given beyond the time limit, even if the answer is correct.

The player who earns 20 points first wins.

Lesson 3.1 Activity
Student Recording Sheet

Round	Card 1	Operation	Card 2	My answer	Correct answer	My score
Example	5	÷	$\frac{4}{5}$	$6\frac{1}{4}$	$6\frac{1}{4}$	2
1						
2						
3						
4						
5						
6						
7						
8						
9						
10						
11						
12						
13						
14						
15						
					Total Score	

Self-Assessment

Which operations involving fractions and mixed numbers did you perform well?

Which operations do you need to practice more? Why do you think so?

9	12	3
15	5	8
11	3	6

18	$\dfrac{1}{5}$	$\dfrac{2}{5}$
$\dfrac{3}{5}$	$\dfrac{4}{5}$	$\dfrac{1}{4}$
$\dfrac{3}{4}$	$\dfrac{2}{3}$	$\dfrac{1}{3}$

$\dfrac{1}{2}$	$\dfrac{5}{6}$	$2\dfrac{1}{4}$
$7\dfrac{1}{4}$	$9\dfrac{2}{3}$	$1\dfrac{2}{3}$
$1\dfrac{3}{4}$	$5\dfrac{1}{2}$	$4\dfrac{1}{2}$

Lesson 3.1 Activity continued
Materials

$8\dfrac{1}{2}$	$4\dfrac{1}{2}$	$3\dfrac{2}{3}$
$+$	$+$	$+$
$+$	$+$	$-$

Lesson 3.1 Activity continued
Materials

—	—	—
—	✕	✕
✕	✕	✕

Lesson 3.1 Activity continued
Materials

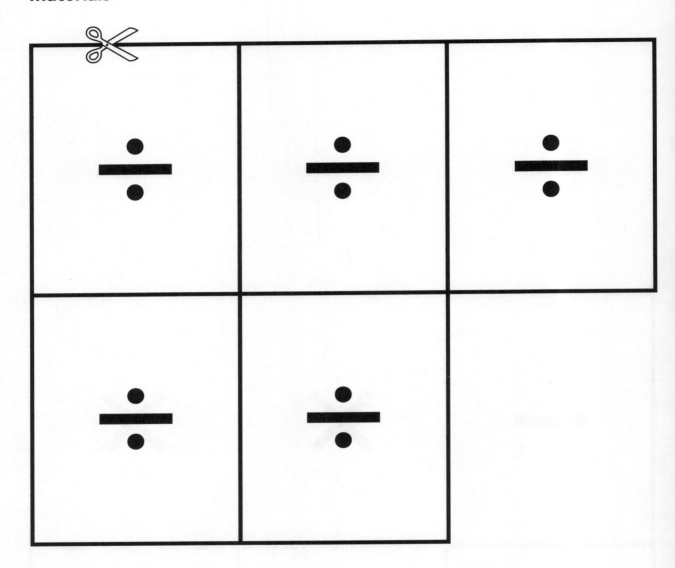

Lessons 3.2–3.3 Activity: Multiplying and Dividing Decimals

Teacher's Guide

Type of activity	Foundational activities for students needing extra help
Objective	Reinforce the skills of multiplying and dividing decimals and solving problems involving multiplication and division of decimals.
Materials	Pencil and paper
Time	20–30 min
Ability levels	Mixed
Prerequisite skills	Multiply and divide decimals.
Grouping	Students should work with a partner.
Assessment of students' learning	See Lesson 3.3 Activity: Rubric.

Lessons 3.2–3.3 Activity Rubric

Category	4	3	2	1
Mathematical concepts	Explanation shows complete understanding of the mathematical concepts used to solve the problem(s).	Explanation shows substantial understanding of the mathematical concepts used to solve the problem(s).	Explanation shows some understanding of the mathematical concepts needed to solve the problem(s).	Explanation shows very limited understanding of the underlying concepts needed to solve the problem(s) OR is not written.
Strategy/ Procedures	Typically uses an efficient and effective strategy to solve the problem(s).	Typically uses an effective strategy to solve the problem(s).	Sometimes uses an effective strategy to solve the problem(s), but does not do it consistently.	Rarely uses an effective strategy to solve the problem(s).
Presentation	Presentation of mathematical calculations is detailed and clear.	Presentation of mathematical calculations is clear.	Presentation of mathematical calculations is a little difficult to understand, but includes critical components.	Presentation of mathematical calculations is difficult to understand and is missing several components OR is not included.

Name: _____   Date: _____

Lessons 3.2–3.3 Activity
Multiplying and Dividing Decimals

An art teacher needs to buy supplies for a class. Here are the costs of some of the items that the teacher needs.

Paintbrushes
5 brushes for $33.95

Watercolor paint
18 colors for $5.22

Paper
$28.75 for 125 sheets

Drawing pencils
12 pencils for $8.52

Clay
$16.50 for 50 lb

Ceramic glaze
4 oz for $3.08

Answer these questions.

1. How much will it cost to buy the following?
   - 45 pounds of clay
   - 32 ounces of ceramic glaze
   - 150 sheets of paper
   - 20 colors of watercolor paint

2. How many paintbrushes can the teacher buy with $100?
   How many drawing pencils can the teacher buy with $100?

3. The teacher estimates that each student will use 2.5 ounces of ceramic glaze for a sculpture project. How many students can do the project if the teacher buys 48 ounces of ceramic glaze?

4. The teacher buys 45 pounds of clay. A student makes a clay flowerpot using 2.25 pounds of the clay. How many more flowerpots identical to the first one can be made with the rest of the clay?

Lessons 3.2–3.3 Activity
Student Recording Sheet

Answer these questions. Show your work.

1. How much will it cost to buy the following?
   a)   45 pounds of clay

   b)   32 ounces of ceramic glaze

   c)   150 sheets of paper

   d)   20 colors of watercolor paint

2. How many of each item can the teacher buy with $100?
   a)   Paintbrushes

   b)   Drawing pencils

3. How many students can do the sculpture project?

4. How many more identical flowerpots can be made with the rest of the clay?

CHAPTER 3   Multiplying and Dividing Fractions and Decimals

Project: Finding the Largest Possible Area for a Given Perimeter

Teacher's Guide

Common Core	
Common Core State Standard	6.NS.1 Interpret and compute quotients of fractions, and solve word problems involving division of fractions by fractions . . . .
Objective	Multiply and divide fractions to solve a problem involving perimeter.
Material	Calculator (optional)
Time	20–30 min
Ability levels	Advanced
Prerequisite skills	Multiply and divide fractions.
Grouping	Students should work with a partner or in a small group.
Assessment of students' learning	See Chapter 3 Project: Rubric.

Chapter 3 Project Rubric

Category	4	3	2	1
Mathematical concepts	Explanation shows complete understanding of the mathematical concepts used to solve the problem(s).	Explanation shows substantial understanding of the mathematical concepts used to solve the problem(s).	Explanation shows some understanding of the mathematical concepts needed to solve the problem(s).	Explanation shows very limited understanding of the underlying concepts needed to solve the problem(s) OR is not written.
Mathematical reasoning	Uses complex and refined mathematical reasoning.	Uses effective mathematical reasoning.	Shows some evidence of mathematical reasoning.	Shows little evidence of mathematical reasoning.
Strategy/ Procedures	Typically uses an efficient and effective strategy to solve the problem(s).	Typically uses an effective strategy to solve the problem(s).	Sometimes uses an effective strategy to solve the problem(s), but does not do it consistently.	Rarely uses an effective strategy to solve the problem(s).
Working with others	Student was an engaged partner, listening to suggestions of others and working cooperatively throughout the lesson.	Student was an engaged partner but had trouble listening to others and/or working cooperatively.	Student cooperated with others, but needed prompting to stay on task.	Student did not work effectively with others.
Explanation	Explanation is detailed and clear.	Explanation is clear.	Explanation is a little difficult to understand, but includes critical components.	Explanation is difficult to understand and is missing several components OR is not included.
Presentation	Presentation of mathematical calculations is detailed and clear.	Presentation of mathematical calculations is clear.	Presentation of mathematical calculations is a little difficult to understand, but includes critical components.	Presentation of mathematical calculations is difficult to understand and is missing several components OR is not included.

Chapter 3 Project
Finding the Largest Possible Area for a Given Perimeter

James has 66 yards of fencing. Each fence panel is $\frac{3}{4}$ yard long. James wants to fence a rectangular section of his yard.

Answer these questions.

1. What is the largest possible rectangular area he could fence in?

2. How many fence panels will there be on each side of the rectangular area?

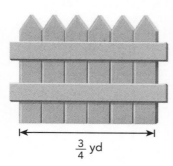

$\frac{3}{4}$ yd

Summarize your findings, and prepare a simple presentation to share in class.

Chapter 3 Project
Student Recording Sheet

1. Describe how you solved the problem. Show any calculations that you made.

Answer these questions.

2. What is the largest possible rectangular area?

3. How many fence panels will there be on each side of the rectangular area?

Ratio

Lesson 4.2 Activity: Equivalent Ratios

Teacher's Guide

Type of activity	Foundational activity for students needing extra help Calculator activity
Objective	Reinforce the skills of writing equivalent ratios, finding missing terms in equivalent terms, and comparing ratios.
Material	Calculator
Time	20–30 min
Ability levels	Mixed
Prerequisite skills	Write ratios to compare two quantities. Write ratios in simplest form. Find the missing term of a pair of equivalent ratios.
Grouping	Students should work with a partner.
Assessment of students' learning	See Lesson 4.2 Activity: Rubric.
Preparation	Depending on the ability of the students, you may consider replacing the sample problems with something easier for the students who need help. Avoid giving too much guidance, as students are encouraged to use the existing problems as their guide. Writing real-world problems serves to reinforce conceptual understanding, and checking accuracy of problems and solutions goes beyond mastery and into the areas of critical analysis, synthesis, and evaluation.

Lesson 4.2 Activity Rubric

Category	4	3	2	1
Mathematical concepts	Explanation shows complete understanding of the mathematical concepts used to solve the problem(s).	Explanation shows substantial understanding of the mathematical concepts used to solve the problem(s).	Explanation shows some understanding of the mathematical concepts needed to solve the problem(s).	Explanation shows very limited understanding of the underlying concepts needed to solve the problem(s) OR is not written.
Mathematical reasoning	Uses complex and refined mathematical reasoning.	Uses effective mathematical reasoning.	Shows some evidence of mathematical reasoning.	Shows little evidence of mathematical reasoning.
Working with others	Student was an engaged partner, listening to suggestions of others and working cooperatively throughout lesson.	Student was an engaged partner but had trouble listening to others and/or working cooperatively.	Student cooperated with others, but needed prompting to stay on task.	Student did not work effectively with others.
Checking	The work is checked by two classmates and all appropriate corrections are made.	The work is checked by one classmate and all appropriate corrections are made.	Work is checked by one classmate but some corrections are not made.	Work is not checked by classmate OR no corrections are made based on feedback.
Neatness and organization	The work is presented in a neat, clear, organized fashion that is easy to read.	The work is presented in a neat and organized fashion that is usually easy to read.	The work is presented in an organized fashion but may be hard to read at times.	The work appears sloppy and unorganized. It is hard to know what information goes together.
Reflection	The reflections show tremendous thought and effort. The learning experience being reflected upon is relevant and meaningful to student and learning goals.	The reflections show considerable thought and effort. Student makes attempts to demonstrate relevance, but the relevance to learning goals is unclear.	The reflections show some thought and effort. Some sections of the reflection are irrelevant to student and/or learning goals.	The reflection is superficial. Most of the reflection is irrelevant to student and/or learning goals.

Lesson 4.2 Activity
Equivalent Ratios

Step 1 Study the real-world problems taken from your textbook and choose one
for this activity.

---

12 The ratio of the weight of vegetables sold to the weight of fruits sold
is 45 : 144.

a) How many times the weight of vegetables sold is the weight of
fruits sold?

b) What fraction of the total weight of vegetables and fruits sold is the
weight of vegetables sold?

---

13 The ratio of the length to the width of a rectangle is 5 : 2.

a) Express the difference between the length and the width of the
rectangle as a fraction of the length of the rectangle.

b) Express the width of the rectangle as a fraction of the perimeter of the
rectangle.

---

35 Judy uses 5 ounces of lemonade concentrate for every 9 ounces of orange
juice concentrate to make a fruit punch.

a) Find the ratio of the number of ounces of orange juice concentrate to
the number of ounces of lemonade concentrate she uses.

b) If Judy uses 36 ounces of orange juice concentrate to make the fruit
punch, how many ounces of lemonade concentrate does she use?

c) If Judy uses 45 ounces of lemonade concentrate to make the fruit punch,
how many ounces of orange juice concentrate does she use?

---

36 In a science experiment, Farah mixed a salt solution and vinegar in the
ratio 3 : 7.

a) If she used 262.8 milliliters of salt solution, how much vinegar did
she use?

b) If 0.56 liter of vinegar was used, how much salt solution did she use?

Lesson 4.2 Activity continued
Equivalent Ratios

Step 2 If you have solved the problem in class, proceed to Step 3. If not, solve the problem you chose and check your solution with your teacher.

Step 3 Write a similar question to the problem you chose. Change the names of the people, objects, activities, numerical values, and so on.

Step 4 Solve the problem and present your solutions clearly. Include an explanation for each step as necessary.

Step 5 Have another pair of students check and refine your work.

Step 6 Make the final changes and submit your work to your teacher. Your teacher will compile and make copies of your work to be made available to the rest of the class.

Lesson 4.2 Activity
Student Recording Sheet

We are modeling problem _____ from the textbook.

Draft of your new problem:

Draft of the detailed solution:

Lesson 4.2 Activity continued
Student Recording Sheet

Revised problem:

Revised detailed solution:

Reflection

What was the most difficult part of this activity? Explain.

Was the statement of the new problem or the solution to the new problem easier for your checkers to figure out? Explain.

CHAPTER 4   Ratio

Project: The Golden Ratio

Teacher's Guide

Common Core	
Common Core State Standard	6.RP.1. . . [U]se ratio language to describe a ratio relationship between two quantities.
Objective	Write ratios involving numbers from the Fibonacci sequence.
Materials	• Ruler • Calculator
Time	20–30 min
Ability levels	Mixed
Prerequisite skill	Write a ratio between two quantities.
Grouping	Students should work with a partner or in a small group.
Assessment of students' learning	See Chapter 4 Project: Rubric.

Chapter 4 Project
Rubric

Category	4	3	2	1
Mathematical concepts	Explanation shows complete understanding of the mathematical concepts used to solve the problem(s).	Explanation shows substantial understanding of the mathematical concepts used to solve the problem(s).	Explanation shows some understanding of the mathematical concepts needed to solve the problem(s).	Explanation shows very limited understanding of the underlying concepts needed to solve the problem(s) OR is not written.
Strategy/ Procedures	Typically uses an efficient and effective strategy to solve the problem(s).	Typically uses an effective strategy to solve the problem(s).	Sometimes uses an effective strategy to solve the problem(s), but does not do it consistently.	Rarely uses an effective strategy to solve the problem(s).
Working with others	Student was an engaged partner, listening to suggestions of others and working cooperatively throughout the lesson.	Student was an engaged partner but had trouble listening to others and/or working cooperatively.	Student cooperated with others, but needed prompting to stay on task.	Student did not work effectively with others.

Chapter 4 Project
The Golden Ratio

The golden ratio is based on the Fibonacci numbers, in which every number in the sequence (after the second) is the sum of the previous two numbers:

1, 1, 2, 3, 5, 8, 13, 21, 34, 55, 89, 144, 233 . . .

Look at the ratio of each number in the Fibonacci sequence to the number before it:

$\frac{1}{1} = 1$ $\frac{2}{1} = 2$ $\frac{3}{2} = 1.5$ $\frac{5}{3} = 1.666\ldots$

$\frac{8}{5} = 1.6$ $\frac{13}{8} = 1.625$ $\frac{21}{13} = 1.61538\ldots$ $\frac{34}{21} = 1.61905\ldots$

$\frac{55}{34} = 1.61764\ldots$ $\frac{89}{55} = 1.61861\ldots$

If we keep going, we will get an interesting number which mathematicians call "phi" (golden ratio): $\Phi = 1.618\ 033\ 988\ 7 \ldots$

Mathematicians, scientists, and naturalists have known this ratio for years. But why is this ratio important? The ratio is said to be "pleasing to the eye" and it is important because it can be found in many areas of life, especially in nature.

For example, the keys in one octave on a piano have 5 black keys, 8 white keys and 13 total keys, yielding two golden ratios: 5 : 8 and 8 : 13. The center of a sunflower and the exterior of a pineapple both exhibit spirals that can be seen to go in two directions. When the ratio of the numbers of spirals in each direction is compared on one of these, it will always be two Fibonacci numbers, and yield a golden ratio.

For this project, you will search for the golden ratio in each item shown on the following pages.

Chapter 4 Project
Student Recording Sheet

1. Find the golden ratio in the Parthenon.

The Parthenon in Greece

Chapter 4 Project continued
Student Recording Sheet

2. Find the golden ratio on your body.

3. Find the golden ratio in the index card.

Chapter 4 Project continued
Student Recording Sheet

4. Find the golden ratio in Pascal's triangle.

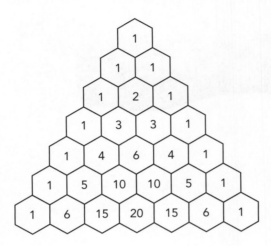

5. Find golden ratios in the 5-pointed star.

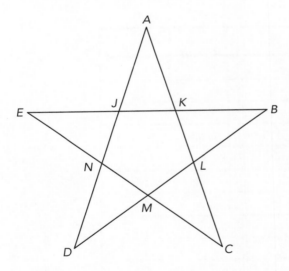

6. Summarize your findings and prepare a simple presentation to share in class.

Rates

Lesson 5.2 Activity: Painting Rooms

Teacher's Guide

Type of activity	Foundational activity for students needing extra help Calculator activity
Objective	Reinforce using rates and unit rates to solve real-world problems.
Material	Calculator
Time	20–30 min
Ability levels	Mixed
Prerequisite skills	Write, simplify, and compare unit rates.
Grouping	Students should work with a partner or in a small group.
Assessment of students' learning	See Lesson 5.2 Activity: Rubric.
Preparation	Discuss with the students how to find the total area of the room to be painted. Suggest that they sketch a rectangular room and label its dimensions, then find the area of each wall and the ceiling.

Lesson 5.2 Activity
Rubric

Category	4	3	2	1
Mathematical concepts	Explanation shows complete understanding of the mathematical concepts used to solve the problem(s).	Explanation shows substantial understanding of the mathematical concepts used to solve the problem(s).	Explanation shows some understanding of the mathematical concepts needed to solve the problem(s).	Explanation shows very limited understanding of the underlying concepts needed to solve the problem(s) OR is not written.
Mathematical reasoning	Uses complex and refined mathematical reasoning.	Uses effective mathematical reasoning.	Shows some evidence of mathematical reasoning.	Shows little evidence of mathematical reasoning.
Working with others	Student was an engaged partner, listening to suggestions of others and working cooperatively throughout the lesson.	Student was an engaged partner but had trouble listening to others and/or working cooperatively.	Student cooperated with others, but needed prompting to stay on task.	Student did not work effectively with others.
Explanation	Explanation is detailed and clear.	Explanation is clear.	Explanation is a little difficult to understand, but includes critical components.	Explanation is difficult to understand and is missing several components OR is not included.
Strategy/ Procedures	Student uses an efficient and effective strategy to solve the problem(s).	Student uses an effective strategy to solve the problem(s).	Student uses an effective strategy to solve the problem(s), but does not do it consistently.	Student does not use an effective strategy to solve the problem(s).

Lesson 5.2 Activity
Painting Rooms

Principal Smith wants to have six classrooms in his school painted as soon as possible. To get the job done quickly, he plans to hire three painters to do the job at the same time.

This table shows the painters' rates.

Painter	Rate per day	Speed	Time available
Junior painter	$140	10 square meters per hour	8 hours/day
Senior painter	$175	15 square meters per hour	8 hours/day

In each room, four walls and the ceiling must be painted, but not the door and the window. This table shows the dimensions of the rooms.

	Room 1	Room 2	Room 3	Room 4	Room 5	Room 6
Length (meters)	6	8	9	9	6	8
Width (meters)	6	6	6	6	6	6
Height (meters)	3	3	3	3	3	3

Each room has one door that is 1 meter wide and 2 meters high, and one window that is 3 meters wide and 2 meters high.

Principal Smith is not sure if he should hire the senior painters or the junior painters. On the Student Recording Sheet, find the possible cost of the painting job for each type of painter. Which type will cost the least amount of money?

Name: _____   Date: _____

Lesson 5.2 Activity
Student Recording Sheet

1. Total area to be painted

Room	Walls	Ceiling	Door	Window	Total area to be painted (square meters)
1			1 × 2 =	2 × 3 =	
2					
3					
4					
5					
6					
				Total	

2. Area each painter can paint in one day

Painter	Speed × hours available	Total area (square meters)
Junior painter		
Senior painter		

3. Costs for three painters to paint the six classrooms

Type of painters	Number of painters	Total area painted per day	How many days needed to paint the total area?	Cost per day	Total cost	Unit rate per square meter
Junior painters	3					
Senior painters	3					

4. Explain how you found the lowest-cost combination of painters for Principal Smith.

CHAPTER 5   Rates

Project: Water Absorption Rate of Different Brands of Paper Towels

Teacher's Guide

Common Core *(Common Core logo)*	
Common Core State Standard	6.RP.3b Solve unit rate problems including those involving . . . constant speed.
Objective	Complete an experiment to test and compare rates of absorption.
Materials	*For each group:* • Set of paper towel strips from at least 3 different brands • Indelible pen • Centimeter ruler • Cup partly filled with colored water • Food coloring • Timer, stop watch, or clock with a second hand
Time	20–30 min
Ability levels	Mixed
Prerequisite skill	Solve unit rate problems.
Grouping	Students should work with a partner or in a small group.
Assessment of students' learning	See Chapter 5 Project: Rubric.
Preparation	Cut different brands of paper towels into 12 cm × 2 cm strips. Label each strip with indelible ink and put them in sets containing one strip from each brand. Try the activity first to make sure that the ink used to label the strips does not bleed or fade when wet. Make sure that the strips are long enough to have a dry portion 20 seconds after being dipped in the water. If the whole strip is wet after 20 seconds, use longer strips or a shorter time. Discuss with the students how to complete Step 2 on the Procedure page. One student should hold the paper strip in the water, and another should act as the timer.

Chapter 5 Project
Rubric

Category	4	3	2	1
Mathematical concepts	Explanation shows complete understanding of the mathematical concepts used to solve the problem(s).	Explanation shows substantial understanding of the mathematical concepts used to solve the problem(s).	Explanation shows some understanding of the mathematical concepts needed to solve the problem(s).	Explanation shows very limited understanding of the underlying concepts needed to solve the problem(s) OR is not written.
Mathematical reasoning	Uses complex and refined mathematical reasoning.	Uses effective mathematical reasoning.	Shows some evidence of mathematical reasoning.	Shows little evidence of mathematical reasoning.
Strategy/ Procedures	Uses an efficient and effective strategy to solve the problem(s).	Uses an effective strategy to solve the problem(s).	Uses an effective strategy to solve the problem(s), but does not do it consistently.	Does not use an effective strategy to solve the problem(s).
Working with others	Student was an engaged partner, listening to suggestions of others and working cooperatively throughout the lesson.	Student was an engaged partner but had trouble listening to others and/or working cooperatively.	Student cooperated with others, but needed prompting to stay on task.	Student did not work effectively with others.
Neatness and organization	The work is presented in a neat, clear, organized fashion that is easy to read.	The work is presented in a neat and organized fashion that is usually easy to read.	The work is presented in an organized fashion but may be hard to read at times.	The work appears sloppy and unorganized. It is hard to know what information goes together.
Explanation	Explanation is detailed and clear.	Explanation is clear.	Explanation is a little difficult to understand, but includes critical components.	Explanation is difficult to understand and is missing several components OR is not included.

Name: _____   Date: _____

Chapter 5 Project
Water Absorption Rate of Different Brands of Paper Towels

In this project, you will set up an experiment to study the water absorption rate of different brands of paper towels. Your group will have at least 3 strips of paper towels of the same length and a cup of colored water.

Step 1 Make sure the strips of paper towels are labeled. Make a mark 2 centimeters from one end of each strip.

Step 2 Hold one strip in the colored water, marked end down, so that the mark you made in Step 1 is level with the water. Continue holding it in the same position for 20 seconds. You may also clip the strip to the side of the cup with a binder clip.

Step 3 When 20 seconds are over, remove the strip of paper towel from the cup. Use a ruler to measure the distance from the end of the strip to the end of the colored portion. Use the Student Recording Sheet to record the length that has absorbed water.

Step 4 Repeat Steps 2 and 3 for each strip.

Step 5 Find the absorption rate for each brand of paper towel. Convert the rate to a unit rate and rank the paper towels starting with the one with the best absorption rate.

Step 6 Use the Student Recording Sheet to summarize your findings and prepare a simple presentation to share in class.

Chapter 5 Project
Student Recording Sheet

1. Describe how you set up the experiment. Include diagrams of the setup.

2. Use the table to record your observations. Convert the rate to a unit rate.
   Show any additional calculations that you made.

Strip	Time (seconds)	Length (centimeters)	Absorption rate
1	20		
2	20		
3	20		
4	20		
5	20		

3. Summarize your findings and draw a conclusion from the experiment.

CHAPTER

6 Percent

Lesson 6.2 Activity: Fractions, Decimals, and Percents

Teacher's Guide

Type of activity	Hands-on activity
Objective	Reinforce the skill of writing equivalent fractions, decimals, and percents.
Materials	Number cards on pages 59–62: • 10 cards with fractions • 10 cards with decimals • 16 cards with percents Timer, stopwatch, or clock with a second hand
Time	20–30 min
Ability levels	Mixed
Prerequisite skills	Express fractions and decimals as percents. Express percents as fractions or decimals.
Grouping	Students should work with a partner.
Assessment of students' learning	See Lesson 6.2 Activity: Rubric.

Lesson 6.2 Activity
Rubric

Category	4	3	2	1
Mathematical concepts	Explanation shows complete understanding of the mathematical concepts used to solve the problem(s).	Explanation shows substantial understanding of the mathematical concepts used to solve the problem(s).	Explanation shows some understanding of the mathematical concepts needed to solve the problem(s).	Explanation shows very limited understanding of the underlying concepts needed to solve the problem(s) OR is not written.
Self-assessment	Self-assessment is accurate and explanation is detailed and clear.	Self-assessment is fairly accurate and explanation is clear.	Self-assessment is inaccurate and explanation is a little difficult to understand, but includes critical components.	Self-assessment is totally inaccurate and explanation is difficult to understand and is missing several components OR is not included.
Reflection	The reflection shows tremendous thought and effort. The learning experience being reflected upon is relevant and meaningful to student and learning goals.	The reflection shows a lot of thought and effort. Student makes attempts to demonstrate relevance, but the relevance is unclear in reference to learning goals.	The reflection shows some thought and effort. Some sections of the reflection is irrelevant to student and/or learning goals.	The reflection is superficial. Most of the reflection is irrelevant to student and/or learning goals.

Lesson 6.2 Activity
Fractions, Decimals, and Percents

Step 1 Players shuffle the stack of cards.

Step 2 Player 1 draws a card from the stack and places it on a table face up.

Step 3 Player 2 has 30 seconds to solve the problem on the card.

Step 4 Player 1 checks the answer. Player 2 keeps the card if he or she solves the problem correctly. If not, the card is placed at the bottom of the pile.

Step 5 Players switch roles and repeat Steps 2 to 4.

Step 6 The player with the most cards after 20 rounds wins.

Lesson 6.2 Activity
Student Recording Sheet

Round	Problem	My answer	Correct answer	Is my answer correct? Yes/No
Example	0.28 → %	28%	28%	Yes
1				
2				
3				
4				
5				
6				
7				
8				
9				
10				
			Total number of correct answers	

Self-Assessment and Reflection

1. In which skill(s) did you do well—expressing fractions as percents, expressing decimals as percents, or expressing percents as fractions or decimals? Explain.

2. In which skill(s) do you need more practice? Why do you think so?

3. What did you learn from this activity?

Lesson 6.2 Activity continued
Materials

Express as a percent. $\dfrac{14}{25}$	Express as a percent. $\dfrac{16}{64}$	Express as a percent. $\dfrac{48}{75}$
Express as a percent. $\dfrac{27}{54}$	Express as a percent. $\dfrac{24}{96}$	Express as a percent. $\dfrac{9}{75}$
Express as a percent. $\dfrac{36}{75}$	Express as a percent. $\dfrac{36}{80}$	Express as a percent. $\dfrac{72}{96}$

Lesson 6.2 Activity continued
Materials

Express as a percent.	Express as a percent.	Express as a percent.
$\dfrac{34}{85}$	0.12	0.56
Express as a percent.	Express as a percent.	Express as a percent.
0.63	0.42	9.8
Express as a percent.	Express as a percent.	Express as a percent.
3	5.0	0.04

Express as a percent.	Express as a percent.	Express as a decimal.
0.7	**2.06**	**55%**
Express as a decimal.	Express as a decimal.	Express as a decimal.
12%	**78%**	**27%**
Express as a decimal.	Express as a decimal.	Express as a decimal.
91%	**42%**	**36%**

Lesson 6.2 Activity continued
Materials

Express as a decimal.	Express as a fraction in simplest form.	Express as a fraction in simplest form.
59%	**35%**	**46%**
Express as a fraction in simplest form.	Express as a fraction in simplest form.	Express as a fraction in simplest form.
76%	**58%**	**82%**
Express as a fraction in simplest form.	Express as a fraction in simplest form.	Express as a fraction in simplest form.
64%	**92%**	**28%**

Lesson 6.3 Activity: Percent of a Quantity

Teacher's Guide

Type of activity	Foundational activities for students needing extra help Calculator activity
Objective	Reinforce the skill of finding the percent of a number.
Materials	Pencil and paper
Time	20–30 min
Ability levels	Mixed
Prerequisite skills	Find the quantity represented by the percent. Find the whole given a quantity and its percent. Find the percent represented by a quantity.
Grouping	Students should work with a partner.
Assessment of students' learning	See Lesson 6.3 Activity: Rubric.

Lesson 6.3 Activity
Rubric

Category	4	3	2	1
Mathematical concepts	Explanation shows complete understanding of the mathematical concepts used to solve the problem(s).	Explanation shows substantial understanding of the mathematical concepts used to solve the problem(s).	Explanation shows some understanding of the mathematical concepts needed to solve the problem(s).	Explanation shows very limited understanding of the underlying concepts needed to solve the problem(s) OR is not written.
Mathematical reasoning	Uses complex and refined mathematical reasoning.	Uses effective mathematical reasoning.	Shows some evidence of mathematical reasoning.	Shows little evidence of mathematical reasoning.
Strategy/ Procedures	Typically uses an efficient and effective strategy to solve the problem(s).	Typically uses an effective strategy to solve the problem(s).	Sometimes uses an effective strategy to solve the problem(s), but does not do it consistently.	Rarely uses an effective strategy to solve the problem(s).
Mathematical errors	90–100% of the steps and solutions have no mathematical errors.	85–89% of the steps and solutions have no mathematical errors.	75–84% of the steps and solutions have no mathematical errors.	More than 25% of the steps and solutions have mathematical errors.

Lesson 6.3 Activity
Percent of a Quantity

A science club used 300 seeds from 7 bean types for a germination experiment. At the end of the experiment, 245 beans germinated. The partially completed table below summarizes the results.

Type of bean	Adzuki bean	Black bean	Black-eyed pea	Soybean	Red bean	?	?
Number of seeds used	50	42	?	75	60	?	?
Number of seeds germinated	?	29	12	?	48	?	?
Percentage of seeds germinated	70%	?	100%	92%	?	?	?

1. Fill in the missing data for the beans listed in the table above. Round to the nearest whole number if necessary.

2. How many of the total number of seeds are not accounted for in this table?

3. Which of the following beans could be the ones that are missing from the table above? Explain.

Type of bean	Mung bean	Great Northern bean	Cranberry bean	Pinto bean	Kidney bean
Number of seeds used	15	30	58	46	61
Number of seeds germinated	12	24	29	40	12
Percentage of seeds germinated	80%	80%	50%	87%	20%

4. Which two bean types had the least percent of germinated beans?

Lesson 6.3 Activity
Student Recording Sheet

1. Fill in the missing data for the beans listed in the table. Show your calculations. Round to the nearest whole number if necessary.

Type of bean	Adzuki bean	Black bean	Black-eyed pea	Soybean	Red bean		
Number of seeds used	50	42		75	60		
Number of seeds germinated		29	12		48		
Percentage of seeds germinated	70%		100%	92%			

Answer these questions.

2. How many of the total number of seeds are not accounted for in the table above?

3. Which bean types could be missing from the table? Complete the table.

4. Which two bean types had the least percent of germinated seeds?

CHAPTER 6   Percent

Project: Coin Flipping

Teacher's Guide

Common Core	
Common Core State Standard	6.RP.3c Find a percent of a quantity as a rate per 100 . . . .
Objective	Express a part of a whole as a percent in order to analyze data from a coin-flipping experiment.
Materials	• Calculator (optional) • Coins: 1 penny, 1 nickel, 1 dime, 1 quarter
Time	20–30 min
Ability levels	Mixed
Prerequisite skill	Write percents.
Grouping	Students should work in groups of four.
Assessment of students' learning	See Chapter 6 Project: Rubric.

Chapter 6 Project
Rubric

Category	4	3	2	1
Mathematical concepts	Explanation shows complete understanding of the mathematical concepts used to solve the problem(s).	Explanation shows substantial understanding of the mathematical concepts used to solve the problem(s).	Explanation shows some understanding of the mathematical concepts needed to solve the problem(s).	Explanation shows very limited understanding of the underlying concepts needed to solve the problem(s) OR is not written.
Strategy/ Procedures	Typically uses an efficient and effective strategy to solve the problem(s).	Typically uses an effective strategy to solve the problem(s).	Sometimes uses an effective strategy to solve the problem(s), but does not do it consistently.	Rarely uses an effective strategy to solve the problem(s).
Working with others	Student was an engaged partner, listening to suggestions of others and working cooperatively throughout the lesson.	Student was an engaged partner but had trouble listening to others and/or working cooperatively.	Student cooperated with others, but needed prompting to stay on task.	Student did not work effectively with others.
Presentation	Presentation of mathematical calculations is detailed and clear.	Presentation of mathematical calculations is clear.	Presentation of mathematical calculations is a little difficult to understand, but includes critical components.	Presentation of mathematical calculations is difficult to understand and is missing several components OR is not included.
Neatness and organization	The work is presented in a neat, clear, organized fashion that is easy to read.	The work is presented in a neat and organized fashion that is usually easy to read.	The work is presented in an organized fashion but may be hard to read at times.	The work appears sloppy and unorganized. It is hard to know what information goes together.
Explanation	Explanation is detailed and clear.	Explanation is clear.	Explanation is a little difficult to understand, but includes critical components.	Explanation is difficult to understand and is missing several components OR is not included.

Chapter 6 Project
Coin Flipping

In this project, you will flip coins to find out

1. if coins land on heads exactly 50% of the time and

2. if different types of coins produce different results.

To help your group make meaningful comparisons, you will be given a penny, a nickel, a dime, and a quarter.

Each member of your group can test a different coin or can take on different roles. Using a single coin at one time, follow the steps below.

Step 1 Flip each coin 10 times for the first round of experiment, 20 times for the second round, and 30 times for the third and final round. As you flip the coin, keep track of the number of times it lands on heads using tally marks.

Step 2 Calculate the percent of flips that the coin landed on heads.

When you have performed the above steps for all the coins, answer the following questions.

1. Did each of the coins land on heads 50% of the time?

2. If it did not, were the percents identical or similar for each round of experiment? What do you think is the reason behind your results?

Summarize your findings and prepare a simple presentation to share in class.

Chapter 6 Project
Student Recording Sheet

1. Describe how your group completed the project.

2. Draw a table to record your data. Show any calculations that you may have.

Answer these questions.

3. Did each of the coins land on heads 50% of the time for each round?

4. If it did not, were the percents identical or similar for each round of experiment? What do you think is the reason behind it?

7 Algebraic Expressions

Lesson 7.1 Activity: Writing Algebraic Expressions for Number Grids

Teacher's Guide

Type of activity	Enrichment activity Calculator activity
Objective	Reinforce the skill of writing algebraic expressions.
Material	Calculator (optional)
Time	20–30 min
Ability levels	Mixed
Prerequisite skill	Write algebraic expressions.
Grouping	Students should work alone or with a partner.
Assessment of students' learning	See Lesson 7.1 Activity: Rubric.
Preparation	The objective of this activity is for students to articulate their thinking process. You may want to discuss with students that this activity will help you assess their thinking about algebraic expressions and help you correct any misconceptions they may have.

Lesson 7.1 Activity
Rubric

Category	4	3	2	1
Mathematical concepts	Explanation shows complete understanding of the mathematical concepts used to solve the problem(s).	Explanation shows substantial understanding of the mathematical concepts used to solve the problem(s).	Explanation shows some understanding of the mathematical concepts needed to solve the problem(s).	Explanation shows very limited understanding of the underlying concepts needed to solve the problem(s) OR is not written.
Mathematical reasoning	Uses complex and refined mathematical reasoning.	Uses effective mathematical reasoning.	Shows some evidence of mathematical reasoning.	Shows little evidence of mathematical reasoning.
Explanation	Explanation is detailed and clear.	Explanation is clear.	Explanation is a little difficult to understand, but includes critical components.	Explanation is difficult to understand and is missing several components OR is not included.
Strategy/ Procedures	Uses an efficient and effective strategy to solve the problem(s).	Uses an effective strategy to solve the problem(s).	Uses an effective strategy to solve the problem(s), but does not do it consistently.	Does not use an effective strategy to solve the problem(s).

Lesson 7.1 Activity
Writing Algebraic Expressions for Number Grids

In this activity, you will write algebraic expressions for the numbers in the grids below. Then use the algebraic rule that you have found to complete the bottom grid.

Before you start, be warned that two boxes in the grids are filled in with the wrong values.

8	23
7	15

12	25
1	13

6	22
11	16

10	4
4	14

4	

Start by putting the grids in order, using the number in the upper left corner as the counter.

What patterns do you notice? Use the Student Recording Sheet to find and record your patterns.

Lesson 7.1 Activity
Student Recording Sheet

1. Put the grids in order, using the number in the upper left corner as the counter. Give each number grid a starting variable, beginning with 1.

6	22
11	16

$x = 1$

8	23
7	15

$x = 2$

10	4
4	14

$x = 3$

12	25
1	13

$x = 4$

Test different algebraic expressions for each square in the grid.
The expressions should transform the starting variable into each number in the grid. Test different expressions with each number grid. Remember that two boxes are incorrect.

2. Write the algebraic rule for a number grid with starting variable x.

3. Test your rule by circling the incorrect values and replacing them with the correct ones. Fill in the missing values for the incomplete grid.

8	23
7	15

12	25
1	13

6	22
11	16

10	4
4	14

4	

Lesson 7.2 Activity: Evaluating Algebraic Expressions: Code Breakers

Teacher's Guide

Type of activity	Foundational activity for students needing extra help Calculator activity
Objective	Reinforce the skill of writing evaluating algebraic expressions.
Material	Calculator (optional)
Time	20–30 min
Ability levels	Mixed
Prerequisite skills	Write and evaluate algebraic expressions.
Grouping	Students should work alone or with a partner.
Assessment of students' learning	See Lesson 7.2 Activity: Rubric.
Preparation	Before beginning the activity, you may want to discuss with students how this type of code works, using a simpler example. For example, use 1 for A, add 10 to get 11, then translate it back to the eleventh letter of the alphabet, K.

Lesson 7.2 Activity Rubric

Category	4	3	2	1
Mathematical concepts	Explanation shows complete understanding of the mathematical concepts used to solve the problem(s).	Explanation shows substantial understanding of the mathematical concepts used to solve the problem(s).	Explanation shows some understanding of the mathematical concepts needed to solve the problem(s).	Explanation shows very limited understanding of the underlying concepts needed to solve the problem(s) OR is not written.
Mathematical reasoning	Uses complex and refined mathematical reasoning.	Uses effective mathematical reasoning.	Shows some evidence of mathematical reasoning.	Shows little evidence of mathematical reasoning.
Explanation	Explanation is detailed and clear.	Explanation is clear.	Explanation is a little difficult to understand, but includes critical components.	Explanation is difficult to understand and is missing several components OR is not included.
Strategy/ Procedures	Uses an efficient and effective strategy to solve the problem(s).	Uses an effective strategy to solve the problem(s).	Uses an effective strategy to solve the problem(s), but does not do it consistently.	Does not use an effective strategy to solve the problem(s).

Lesson 7.2 Activity
Evaluating Algebraic Expressions: Code Breakers

Our intelligence obtained this coded message sent out by a spy agent to his contact.

U M R R F K V S L R T R F E R O D H L V Q R E R O

We captured another agent two weeks ago and picked up a decoding wheel on him. Unfortunately, it is partial and incomplete.

Original	A	B	C	D	E	F	G	H	I	J	K	L	M
Coded	–	–	–	–	–	U	X	A	–	–	J	M	P

Original	N	O	P	Q	R	S	T	U	V	W	X	Y	Z
Coded	S	–	–	–	–	H	–	–	Q	T	W	–	–

We believe that this spy ring translates each letter to a number, using A = 1, B = 2, C = 3, and so on. They then change each number to another number, using a key, and translate the new number back into a letter. Our preliminary analysis of the decoding wheel suggests that an algebraic expression was used as the key.

Help us find the key by applying what you know about algebra and use it to crack the code. (*Hint:* If the key gives you a number greater than 26, subtract 26 to crack the code. For example, if the result of the key is 27, use 27 − 26 = 1, or A, for the letter.)

We have only 20 minutes to crack the code. Make haste!

Lesson 7.2 Activity
Student Recording Sheet

Break the code

1. How did you unlock the key?

2. What pattern did you observe?

3. What did you do to verify that the key is working and correct?

Decode the message

4. What was the message sent out by the agent?

CHAPTER 7   Algebraic Expressions

Project: Using Algebraic Expressions to Identify Patterns in Triangles

Teacher's Guide

Common Core State Standard	6.EE.6 Use variables to represent numbers and write expressions when solving a real-world or mathematical problem . . . .
Objective	Write and use an algebraic expression to express a general rule for a pattern.
Materials	*For each group:* • Calculator (optional) • 30 small counters, coins, or pieces of paper
Time	20–30 min
Ability levels	Mixed
Prerequisite skills	Write and evaluate algebraic expressions.
Grouping	Students should work alone or with a partner.
Assessment of students' learning	See Chapter 7 Project: Rubric.
Preparation	If you do not have a supply of counters, punch circles from sturdy paper or ask students to bring 30 pennies to class.

Chapter 7 Project
Rubric

Category	4	3	2	1
Mathematical concepts	Explanation shows complete understanding of the mathematical concepts used to solve the problem(s).	Explanation shows substantial understanding of the mathematical concepts used to solve the problem(s).	Explanation shows some understanding of the mathematical concepts needed to solve the problem(s).	Explanation shows very limited understanding of the underlying concepts needed to solve the problem(s) OR is not written.
Mathematical reasoning	Uses complex and refined mathematical reasoning.	Uses effective mathematical reasoning.	Shows some evidence of mathematical reasoning.	Shows little evidence of mathematical reasoning.
Strategy/ Procedures	Uses an efficient and effective strategy to solve the problem(s).	Uses an effective strategy to solve the problem(s).	Uses an effective strategy to solve the problem(s), but does not do it consistently.	Does not use an effective strategy to solve the problem(s).
Working with others	Student was an engaged partner, listening to suggestions of others and working cooperatively throughout the lesson.	Student was an engaged partner but had trouble listening to others and/or working cooperatively.	Student cooperated with others, but needed prompting to stay on task.	Student did not work effectively with others.

Chapter 7 Project
Using Algebraic Expressions to Identify Patterns in Triangles

1. Using counters, make triangles of different sizes as shown.

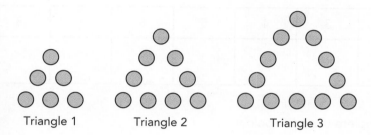

Triangle 1   Triangle 2   Triangle 3

2. Record the number of counters you use to make each triangle. Use the table on the Student Recording Sheet to record your data.

3. Use counters to make five more similar triangles. Record the number of counters you use for each triangle.

4. Study the table carefully and write a formula for finding the number of counters needed to form Triangle n.

5. Using your formula, find how many counters will be used to form Triangle 175 and Triangle 200.

6. Summarize your results. Prepare to share them in class.

Chapter 7 Project
Student Recording Sheet

1. Record your data in the table below.

Triangle	1	2	3	4	5	6	7	8
Number of counters	6	9						

2. Use your results from Step 1 to complete the table below.

Triangle	Difference in the number of counters used from the previous triangle	Pattern formed	Number of counters used
1	–	–	6
2	3	3 × 2 + 3	9
3	3		
4			
5			
6			
7			
8			

3. Write a formula for the number of counters needed to form Triangle *n*.

4. How many counters will you need to form Triangle 175? Triangle 200?

5. Summarize your results and write a conclusion for the activity.

Equations and Inequalities

Lesson 8.2 Activity: Writing and Solving Linear Equations

Teacher's Guide

Type of activity	Foundational activity for students needing extra help Calculator activity
Objective	Reinforce the skills of expressing the relationship between two quantities as a linear equation and using a table or graph to represent a linear equation.
Material	Calculator
Time	20–30 min
Ability levels	Mixed
Prerequisite skills	Write a linear equation to represent a given situation. Use tables and graphs to represent linear equations.
Grouping	Students should work with a partner.
Assessment of students' learning	See Lesson 8.2 Activity: Rubric.
Preparation	In this activity, students will write their own word problems, based on examples in the textbook. Depending on the ability of the students, you may want to replace one or more of the sample problems with a simpler example. Avoid giving too much guidance, as students are encouraged to use the existing problems as their guide. Writing real-world problems reinforces conceptual understanding, and checking accuracy of problems and solutions goes beyond mastery and into the areas of critical analysis, synthesis, and evaluation. You may want to compile and make copies of the students' problems and make them available to the whole class.

Lesson 8.2 Activity
Rubric

Category	4	3	2	1
Mathematical concepts	Explanation shows complete understanding of the mathematical concepts used to solve the problem(s).	Explanation shows substantial understanding of the mathematical concepts used to solve the problem(s).	Explanation shows some understanding of the mathematical concepts needed to solve the problem(s).	Explanation shows very limited understanding of the underlying concepts needed to solve the problem(s) OR is not written.
Mathematical reasoning	Uses complex and refined mathematical reasoning.	Uses effective mathematical reasoning.	Shows some evidence of mathematical reasoning.	Shows little evidence of mathematical reasoning.
Working with others	Student was an engaged partner, listening to suggestions of others and working cooperatively throughout lesson.	Student was an engaged partner but had trouble listening to others and/or working cooperatively.	Student cooperated with others, but needed prompting to stay on task.	Student did not work effectively with others.
Checking	The work is checked by two classmates and all appropriate corrections are made.	The work is checked by one classmate and all appropriate corrections are made.	Work is checked by one classmate but some corrections are not made.	Work is not checked by classmate OR no corrections are made based on feedback.
Neatness and organization	The work is presented in a neat, clear, organized fashion that is easy to read.	The work is presented in a neat and organized fashion that is usually easy to read.	The work is presented in an organized fashion but may be hard to read at times.	The work appears sloppy and unorganized. It is hard to know what information goes together.
Reflection	The reflections show tremendous thought and effort. The learning experience being reflected upon is relevant and meaningful to student and learning goals.	The reflections show considerable thought and effort. Student makes attempts to demonstrate relevance, but the relevance to learning goals is unclear.	The reflections show some thought and effort. Some sections of the reflection are irrelevant to student and/or learning goals.	The reflection is superficial. Most of the reflection is irrelevant to student and/or learning goals.

Lesson 8.2 Activity
Writing and Solving Linear Equations

Step 1 Read these problems from your textbook and choose one for this activity.

---

5 Ethan scored x points in a game. His younger sister scored 8 points when she played the same game. Their combined score was y points.

a) Write an equation relating x and y.

b) Copy and complete the table to show the relationship between x and y.

Ethan's scores (x points)	10	11	12	13	14	15
Combined scores (y points)	?	?	?	?	?	?

---

6 There are x sparrows in a tree. There are 50 sparrows on the ground beneath the tree. Let y represent the total number of sparrows in the tree and on the ground.

a) Express y in terms of x.

b) Make a table to show the relationship between y and x. Use values of $x = 10, 20, 30, 40,$ and 50 in your table.

c) Graph the relationship between y and x on a coordinate plane.

---

7 A rectangle has a perimeter of P centimeters. Its width is b centimeters. Its length is double its width.

a) Express P in terms of b.

b) Copy and complete the table to show the relationship between P and b.

Width (b centimeters)	1	2	3	4	5	6
Perimeter (P centimeters)	?	?	?	?	?	?

Lesson 8.2 Activity continued
Writing and Solving Linear Equations

8 Every month, Amaan spends 60% of what he earns and saves the rest. Amaan earns n dollars and saves r dollars each month.

a) Express r in terms of n.

b) Make a table to show the relationship between r and n. Use values of $n = 100, 200, 400,$ and 500 in your table.

c) Graph the relationship between n and r on a coordinate plane.

d) The point $(287.5, 115)$ is on the line you drew in **c)**. Does this point make sense in the situation? Explain.

Step 2 If you have already solved the problem in class, go to Step 3. If not, solve the problem you chose and check your solution with your teacher.

Step 3 Write a question that is similar to the problem you chose. Change the names of the people, objects, activities, numerical values, and so on.

Step 4 Solve the new problem and present your solutions clearly. Include an explanation for each step as necessary.

Step 5 Have another pair of students check your work and make suggestions for improving it.

Step 6 Make any final changes.

Lesson 8.2 Activity
Student Recording Sheet

We are modeling problem _____ from the textbook.

Draft of your new problem:

Draft of the detailed solution:

Lesson 8.2 Activity continued
Student Recording Sheet

Revised problem:

Revised detailed solution:

Reflection

What was the most difficult part of this activity? Explain.

CHAPTER 8   Equations and Inequalities

Project: Planning a Healthy Meal

Teacher's Guide

Common Core	
Common Core State Standard	6.EE.5 . . . Use substitution to determine whether a given number in a specified set makes an . . . inequality true.
Objective	Practice working with inequalities.
Materials	• Calculator • List of Food Items on pages 93–100
Time	20–30 min
Ability levels	Mixed
Prerequisite skill	Determine solutions of inequalities of the forms $x \geq c$ and $x \leq c$.
Grouping	Students should work with a partner or in a small group.
Assessment of students' learning	See Chapter 8 Project: Rubric.

Chapter 8 Project
Rubric

Category	4	3	2	1
Mathematical concepts	Explanation shows complete understanding of the mathematical concepts used to solve the problem(s).	Explanation shows substantial understanding of the mathematical concepts used to solve the problem(s).	Explanation shows some understanding of the mathematical concepts needed to solve the problem(s).	Explanation shows very limited understanding of the underlying concepts needed to solve the problem(s) OR is not written.
Mathematical reasoning	Uses complex and refined mathematical reasoning.	Uses effective mathematical reasoning.	Shows some evidence of mathematical reasoning.	Shows little evidence of mathematical reasoning.
Strategy/ Procedures	Uses an efficient and effective strategy to solve the problem(s).	Uses an effective strategy to solve the problem(s).	Uses an effective strategy to solve the problem(s), but does not do it consistently.	Does not use an effective strategy to solve the problem(s).
Working with others	Student was an engaged partner, listening to suggestions of others and working cooperatively throughout the lesson.	Student was an engaged partner but had trouble listening to others and/or working cooperatively.	Student cooperated with others, but needed prompting to stay on task.	Student did not work effectively with others.

Chapter 8 Project
Planning a Healthy Meal

For this project, you will be planning a healthy, well-balanced meal made up of a soup, a main dish, and a dessert. Your meal must include the four main food groups of grains, vegetables, fruits, and meat and satisfy the following requirements:

- Total calories (a)   : $600 \leq a \leq 800$
- Total fat (b)   : $b \leq 35\%$ of total calories
- Lean meat/beans (c)   : $c \leq 2$ ounces
- Fruits (d)   : $d \leq 0.5$ cup
- Vegetables (e)   : $0.5 \text{ cup} \leq e \leq 0.7 \text{ cup}$
- Grain (f)   : $f \leq 2$ ounces

You will use a list of food items and their nutritional values. If any information you need is not available on the list, you can estimate or calculate the information. For example, to find the amount of fat in one-eighth of a cake, you can divide the value for the total fat by 8.

Here are some useful conversions:
- 1 gram of fat = 9 calories
- 1 ounce = 28.35 grams
- 1 cup = 128 grams

When you are finished, be prepared to explain how you selected food items to create a healthy, well-balanced meal.

Chapter 8 Project
Student Recording Sheet

Use the table(s) to record your choices. Show all your work.

Soup

Description of food	Food group	Quantity	Fat (grams)	Food energy (calories)

Main Dish

Description of food	Food group	Quantity	Fat (grams)	Food energy (calories)

Dessert

Description of food	Food group	Quantity	Fat (grams)	Food energy (calories)

Chapter 8 Project continued
List of Food Items

Description of food		Fat (Grams)	Food energy (Calories)	Weight (Grams)
1,000 Island, Salad Dressing	1 tablespoon	6	60	16
Almonds, Whole	1 ounce	15	165	28
Apples, Raw	1 apple	1	125	212
Apple Juice	1 cup	0	115	248
Apple Pie	1 pie	105	2,420	945
Apricots	3 apricots	0	50	106
Artichokes	1 artichoke	0	55	120
Asparagus	1 cup	1	45	180
Avocados	1 avocado	30	305	173
Bananas	1 banana	1	105	114
Barbecue Sauce	1 tablespoon	0	10	16
Barley	1 cup	2	700	200
Bean Sprouts	1 cup	0	25	124
Beef and Vegetable Stew	1 cup	11	220	245
Beef Broth	1 cup	1	15	240
Beef Gravy	1 cup	5	125	233
Beef Liver, Fried	3 ounces	7	185	85
Beef Noodle Soup	1 cup	3	85	244
Beef Potpie	1 piece	30	515	210
Beef Roast	3 ounces	26	315	85
Beef Steak	3 ounces	15	240	85
Beef, Corned	3 ounces	10	185	85
Beet Greens	1 cup	0	40	144
Beets	2 beets	0	30	100
Black Beans	1 cup	1	225	171
Black-Eyed Peas	1 cup	1	190	250
Blackberries, Raw	1 cup	1	75	144
Blueberries, Raw	1 cup	1	80	145
Blueberry Muffins	1 muffin	5	140	45
Blueberry Pie	1 pie	102	2,285	945
Boston Brown Bread	1 slice	1	95	45
Bran Muffins	1 muffin	4	140	45
Broccoli	1 cup	0	50	185
Brownies with Nuts	1 brownie	4	100	25
Brussels Sprouts	1 cup	1	65	155
Butter	1 tablespoon	11	100	14
Cabbage, Common	1 cup	0	30	150
Cantaloup, Raw	half melon	1	95	267
Caramels	1 ounce	3	115	28
Carrot Cake	1 cake	328	6,175	1,536
Carrots, Cooked	1 cup	0	70	156
Cashew Nuts, Oil Roasted	1 ounce	14	165	28

Chapter 8 Project continued
List of Food Items

Description of food		Fat (Grams)	Food energy (Calories)	Weight (Grams)
Catsup	1 tablespoon	0	15	15
Cauliflower	1 cup	0	35	180
Celery Seed	1 teaspoon	1	10	2
Celery, Pascal Type	1 cup	0	20	120
Cheddar Cheese	1 ounce	9	115	28
Cheeseburger, 4-ounce Patty	1 sandwich	31	525	194
Cheeseburger, Regular	1 sandwich	15	300	112
Cheesecake	1 cake	213	3,350	1,110
Cherries	10 cherries	1	50	68
Cherry Pie	1 pie	107	2,465	945
Chestnuts, European, Roasted	1 cup	3	350	143
Chicken a la King	1 cup	34	470	245
Chicken and Noodles	1 cup	18	365	240
Chicken Chow Mein	1 cup	10	255	250
Chicken Frankfurter	1 frank	9	115	45
Chicken Gravy	1 cup	14	190	238
Chicken Liver, Cooked	1 liver	1	30	20
Chicken Noodle Soup	1 cup	2	75	241
Chicken Potpie	1 piece	31	545	232
Chicken Roll, Light	2 slices	4	90	57
Chicken, Fried, Batter, Breast	4.9 ounces	18	365	140
Chicken, Fried, Batter, Drumstick	2.5 ounces	11	195	72
Chicken, Fried, Flour, Breast	3.5 ounces	9	220	98
Chicken, Fried, Flour, Drumstick	1.7 ounces	7	120	49
Chicken, Roasted, Breast	3.0 ounces	3	140	86
Chicken, Roasted, Drumstick	1.6 ounces	2	75	44
Chicken, Stewed	1 cup	9	250	140
Chickpeas	1 cup	4	270	163
Chili Con Carne with Beans	1 cup	16	340	255
Chocolate Chip Cookies	4 cookies	11	225	48
Chop Suey with Beef and Pork	1 cup	17	300	250
Cinnamon	1 teaspoon	0	5	2
Clam Chowder, with Milk	1 cup	7	165	248
Clams	3 ounces	2	85	85
Coconut, Dried, Sweetened, Shredded	1 cup	33	470	93
Coconut, Raw	1 piece	15	160	45
Coconut, Raw, Shredded	1 cup	27	285	80
Coffeecake	1 cake	41	1,385	430
Cooked Salad Dressing	1 tablespoon	2	25	16

Chapter 8 Project continued
List of Food Items

Description of food		Fat (Grams)	Food energy (Calories)	Weight (Grams)
Corn Muffins	1 muffin	6	145	45
Corn, White	1 ear	0	60	63
Corn, Yellow	1 ear	1	85	77
Cottage Cheese, Creamed	1 cup	10	235	225
Cottage Cheese, Uncreamed	1 cup	1	125	145
Cream of Chicken Soup	1 cup	11	190	248
Cream of Mushroom Soup	1 cup	14	205	248
Crabmeat	1 cup	3	135	135
Cracked-Wheat Bread	1 slice	1	65	25
Cranberry Juice	1 cup	0	145	253
Cranberry Sauce	1 cup	0	420	277
Cream Cheese	1 ounce	10	100	28
Cucumber	6 slices	0	5	28
Custard Pie	1 pie	101	1,985	910
Custard, Baked	1 cup	15	305	265
Dates	10 dates	0	230	83
Duck, Roasted	half duck	25	445	221
Eggnog	1 cup	19	340	254
Eggplant, Steamed	1 cup	0	25	96
Eggs, Fried	1 egg	7	90	46
Eggs, Hard-Cooked	1 egg	5	75	50
Eggs, Poached	1 egg	5	75	50
Eggs, Scrambled/Omelet	1 egg	7	100	61
Eggs, Raw, White	1 white	0	15	33
Eggs, Raw, Whole	1 egg	5	75	50
Eggs, Raw, Yolk	1 yolk	5	60	17
Enchilada	1 enchilada	16	235	230
English Muffin, Egg, Cheese, Bacon	1 sandwich	18	360	138
English Muffin, Plain	1 muffin	1	140	57
Evaporated Milk, Skim	1 cup	1	200	255
Evaporated Milk, Whole	1 cup	19	340	252
Feta Cheese	1 ounce	6	75	28
Fish Sandwich with Cheese	1 sandwich	23	420	140
Fish Sticks	1 stick	3	70	28
Flounder or Sole, Baked	3 ounces	6	120	85
Frankfurter	1 frank	13	145	45
French Bread	1 slice	1	100	35
French Salad Dressing	1 tablespoon	9	85	16
Fried Pie, Apple or Cherry	1 pie	14	255	85
Fruitcake	1 cake	228	5,185	1,361
Gelatin Dessert	1 cup	0	140	240

Chapter 8 Project continued
List of Food Items

Description of food		Fat (Grams)	Food energy (Calories)	Weight (Grams)
Gingerbread Cake	1 cake	39	1,575	570
Grapefruit Juice, Sweetened	1 cup	0	115	250
Grapefruit Juice, Unsweetened	1 cup	0	95	247
Grapefruit, Raw	1 fruit	0	80	240
Grapes, European, Raw	10 grapes	0	40	57
Gravy and Turkey	5 ounces	4	95	142
Ground Beef, Broiled	3 ounces	18	245	85
Haddock, Breaded, Fried	3 ounces	9	175	85
Halibut, Broiled, Butter	3 ounces	6	140	85
Hamburger, 4-ounce Patty	1 sandwich	21	445	174
Hamburger, Regular	1 sandwich	11	245	98
Herring, Pickled	3 ounces	13	190	85
Hollandaise Sauce	1 cup	20	240	259
Honey	1 tablespoon	0	65	21
Honeydew Melon, Raw	1/10 melon	0	45	129
Italian Bread	1 slice	0	85	30
Italian Salad Dressing	1 tablespoon	9	80	15
Jams and Preserves	1 tablespoon	0	55	20
Kale	1 cup	1	40	130
Kiwifruit, Raw	1 kiwi	0	45	76
Lamb, Rib, Roasted	3 ounces	26	315	85
Lamb, Chops, Arm, Braised	2.2 ounces	15	220	63
Lamb, Chops, Loin, Broiled	2.8 ounces	16	235	80
Lamb, Leg, Roasted	3 ounces	13	205	85
Lemon Juice	1 cup	1	50	244
Lemon Meringue Pie	1 pie	86	2,140	840
Lemonade, Concentrate	6 fluid ounces	0	425	219
Lettuce, Butterhead, Raw, Leaves	1 leaf	0	0	15
Lettuce, Crisphead, Raw, Pieces	1 cup	0	5	55
Lettuce, Looseleaf	1 cup	0	10	56
Lime Juice	1 cup	1	50	246
Macadamia Nuts, Oil Roasted	1 ounce	22	205	28
Macaroni and Cheese	1 cup	10	230	240
Macaroni, Cooked	1 cup	1	190	130
Mangos, Raw	1 mango	1	135	207
Margarine	1 tablespoon	11	100	14
Mayonnaise	1 tablespoon	11	100	14
Milk, Low Fat	1 cup	5	125	245
Milk, Skim	1 cup	1	90	245
Milk, Whole	1 cup	8	150	244

Chapter 8 Project continued
List of Food Items

Description of food			Fat (Grams)	Food energy (Calories)	Weight (Grams)
Minestrone Soup	1 cup		3	80	241
Miso	1 cup		13	470	276
Mixed Grain Bread	1 slice		1	65	25
Mixed Nuts	1 ounce		16	175	28
Mozzarella Cheese, Whole Milk	1 ounce		6	80	28
Mozzarella Cheese, Skim	1 ounce		5	80	28
Mushroom Gravy	1 cup		6	120	238
Mushrooms	1 cup		1	40	156
Mustard Greens	1 cup		0	20	140
Mustard, Yellow	1 teaspoon		0	5	5
Noodles, Chow Mein, Canned	1 cup		11	220	45
Noodles, Egg	1 cup		2	200	160
Oatmeal Bread	1 slice		1	65	25
Oatmeal with Raisins Cookies	4 cookies		10	245	52
Ocean Perch, Breaded, Fried	1 fillet		11	185	85
Olives, Green	4 medium		2	15	13
Olives, Ripe	3 small		2	15	9
Onion Powder	1 teaspoon		0	5	2
Onion Rings, Breaded	2 rings		5	80	20
Orange Juice	1 cup		0	110	248
Oranges, Raw	1 orange		0	60	131
Oysters, Breaded, Fried	1 oyster		5	90	45
Oysters	1 cup		4	160	240
Pancakes, Plain	1 pancake		2	60	27
Papayas, Raw	1 cup		0	65	140
Parmesan Cheese, Grated	1 tablespoon		2	25	5
Parsley, Raw	10 sprigs		0	5	10
Peach Pie	1 pie		101	2,410	945
Peaches, Raw	1 peach		0	35	87
Peanut Butter	1 tablespoon		8	95	16
Peanut Butter Cookies	4 cookies		14	245	48
Peanuts, Oil Roasted	1 ounce		14	165	28
Pears, Raw, Bartlett	1 pear		1	100	166
Peas, Green	1 cup		1	115	170
Pecan Pie	1 pie		189	3,450	825
Pecans, Halves	1 ounce		19	190	28
Peppers, Sweet, Cooked	1 pepper		0	15	73
Peppers, Sweet, Raw	1 pepper		0	20	74
Pickles, Cucumber, Dill	1 pickle		0	5	65
Pickles, Cucumber, Fresh Pack	2 slices		0	10	15

Chapter 8 Project continued
List of Food Items

Description of food		Fat (Grams)	Food energy (Calories)	Weight (Grams)
Pickles, Cucumber, Sweet Gherkin	1 pickle	0	20	15
Pineapple Juice	1 cup	0	140	250
Pineapple, Canned, Heavy Syrup	1 cup	0	200	255
Pineapple, Canned, Juice Pack	1 cup	0	150	250
Pineapple, Raw, Diced	1 cup	1	75	155
Pita Bread	1 pita	1	165	60
Plantains, Cooked	1 cup	0	180	154
Plums, Canned, Heavy Syrup	1 cup	0	230	258
Plums, Canned, Juice Pack	1 cup	0	145	252
Plums, Raw	1 plum	0	35	66
Pork Chop, Loin, Broiled	3.1 ounces	19	275	87
Pork Chop, Loin, Pan-fried	3.1 ounces	27	335	89
Pork Fresh Ham, Roasted	3 ounces	18	250	85
Pork Fresh Rib, Roasted	3 ounces	20	270	85
Pork Shoulder, Braised	3 ounces	22	295	85
Pork, Cured, Bacon	3 slices	9	110	19
Pork, Cured, Ham, Roasted	3 ounces	14	205	85
Pork, Link, Cooked	1 link	4	50	13
Pork, Luncheon Meat, Canned	2 slices	13	140	42
Potato Salad with Mayonnaise	1 cup	21	360	250
Potatoes, Baked	1 potato	0	220	202
Potatoes, Boiled	1 potato	0	120	136
Potatoes, Hash Brown	1 cup	18	340	156
Potatoes, Mashed	1 cup	12	235	210
Potatoes, Scalloped	1 cup	9	210	245
Potatoes, French Fries	10 strips	8	160	50
Prune Juice, Canned	1 cup	0	180	256
Prunes, Dried	5 large	0	115	49
Pudding, Chocolate	5 ounces	11	205	142
Pudding, Rice	half cup	4	155	132
Pudding, Tapioca	5 ounces	5	160	142
Pudding, Vanilla	5 ounces	10	220	142
Pumpkin and Squash Kernels	1 ounce	13	155	28
Pumpkin Pie	1 pie	102	1,920	910
Pumpkin, Canned	1 cup	1	85	245
Radish, Raw	4 radishes	0	5	18
Raisin Bread	1 slice	1	65	25
Raspberries, Raw	1 cup	1	60	123
Relish, Sweet	1 tablespoon	0	20	15
Rice, Brown	1 cup	1	230	195

Chapter 8 Project continued
List of Food Items

Description of food		Fat (Grams)	Food energy (Calories)	Weight (Grams)
Rice, White	1 cup	0	225	205
Roast Beef Sandwich	1 sandwich	13	345	150
Rolls, Dinner	1 roll	2	85	28
Rolls, Frankfurter and Hamburger	1 roll	2	115	40
Rolls, Hoagie or Submarine	1 roll	8	400	135
Rye Bread, Light	1 slice	1	65	25
Salmon, Baked, Red	3 ounces	5	140	85
Salmon, Canned, Pink	3 ounces	5	120	85
Salmon, Smoked	3 ounces	8	150	85
Sardines, Atlantic	3 ounces	9	175	85
Scallops, Breaded	6 scallops	10	195	90
Sesame Seeds	1 tablespoon	4	45	8
Sour Cream	1 tablespoon	3	25	12
Soy Sauce	1 tablespoon	0	10	18
Spaghetti, Cooked, Firm	1 cup	1	190	130
Spaghetti, Cooked, Tender	1 cup	1	155	140
Spaghetti, Tomato Sauce with Cheese	1 cup	9	260	250
Spaghetti, Meatballs, Tomato Sauce	1 cup	12	330	248
Spinach Souffle	1 cup	18	220	136
Spinach, Cooked From Raw	1 cup	0	40	180
Squash, Summer, Cooked	1 cup	1	35	180
Squash, Winter, Baked	1 cup	1	80	205
Strawberries, Frozen, Sweetend	10 ounces	0	275	284
Strawberries, Raw	1 cup	1	45	149
Sugar, Brown	1 cup	0	820	220
Sugar, White, Granulated	1 cup	0	770	200
Sweet (Dark) Chocolate	1 ounce	10	150	28
Sweet potato, Baked	1 potato	0	115	114
Sweet potato, Boiled	1 potato	0	160	151
Swiss Cheese	1 ounce	8	105	28
Tangerine Juice	1 cup	0	125	249
Tangerines, Raw	1 tangerine	0	35	84
Tartar Sauce	1 tablespoon	8	75	14
Tofu	1 piece	5	85	120
Tomato Juice	1 cup	0	40	244
Tomato Paste	1 cup	2	220	262
Tomato Sauce	1 cup	0	75	245
Tomato Vegetable Soup	1 packet	1	40	189

Chapter 8 Project continued
List of Food Items

Description of food		Fat (Grams)	Food energy (Calories)	Weight (Grams)
Tomatoes, Raw	1 tomato	0	25	123
Trout, Broiled, with Butter	3 ounces	9	175	85
Tuna Salad	1 cup	19	375	205
Tuna, Canned, Drained, Oil, Light	3 ounces	7	165	85
Tuna, Canned, Drained, Water, White	3 ounces	1	135	85
Turkey Ham, Cured Turkey Thigh	2 slices	3	75	57
Turkey Loaf, Breast Meat	2 slices	1	45	42
Turkey Patties	1 patty	12	180	64
Turkey, Roasted, Light + Dark	1 cup	7	240	140
Turnip Greens	1 cup	1	50	164
Turnips	1 cup	0	30	156
Veal Cutlet, Medium Fat	3 ounces	9	185	85
Veal Rib, Medium Fat	3 ounces	14	230	85
Vegetable Beef Soup, Canned	1 cup	2	80	244
Vegetables, Mixed	1 cup	0	105	182
Vegetarian Soup	1 cup	2	70	241
Vienna Bread	1 slice	1	70	25
Vienna Sausage	1 sausage	4	45	16
Vinegar and Oil Salad Dressing	1 tablespoon	8	70	16
Vinegar, Cider	1 tablespoon	0	0	15
Walnuts	1 ounce	18	180	28
Water Chestnuts, Canned	1 cup	0	70	140
Watermelon, Raw, Diced	1 cup	1	50	160
Wheat Bread	1 slice	1	65	25
White Bread	1 slice	1	55	20
Whole-Wheat Bread	1 slice	1	70	28

Reference:
U.S. Department of Agriculture, Agricultural Research Service. 2010.
USDA National Nutrient Database for Standard Reference, Release 23.
Nutrient Data Laboratory Home Page, http://www.ars.usda.gov/nutrientdata

The Coordinate Plane

Lesson 9.1 Activity: Coordinate Plane Treasure Hunt

Teacher's Guide

Type of activity	Hands-on activity
Objective	Reinforce the skills of naming and locating points on the coordinate plane.
Material	Treasure hunt grid paper on page 106
Time	20–30 min
Ability levels	Mixed
Prerequisite skill	Find the coordinates of points on a coordinate plane.
Grouping	Students should work with a partner.
Assessment of students' learning	See Lesson 9.1 Activity: Rubric.
Preparation	Make more than one copy of the Treasure Hunt grid (page 106) for each student, as they may have time to play the game more than once.

Lesson 9.1 Activity
Rubric

Category	4	3	2	1
Strategy/ Procedures	Typically uses an efficient and effective strategy to solve the problem(s).	Typically uses an effective strategy to solve the problem(s).	Sometimes uses an effective strategy to solve problems, but does not do it consistently.	Rarely uses an effective strategy to solve problems.
Mathematical reasoning	Uses complex and refined mathematical reasoning.	Uses effective mathematical reasoning.	Shows some evidence of mathematical reasoning.	Shows little evidence of mathematical reasoning.
Explanation	Explanation is detailed and clear.	Explanation is clear.	Explanation is a little difficult to understand, but includes critical components.	Explanation is difficult to understand and is missing several components OR is not included.
Reflection	The reflections show tremendous thought and effort. The learning experience being reflected upon is relevant and meaningful to student and learning goals.	The reflections show considerable thought and effort. Student makes attempts to demonstrate relevance, but the relevance to learning goals is unclear.	The reflections show some thought and effort. Some sections of the reflection are irrelevant to student and/or learning goals.	The reflection is superficial. Most of the reflection is irrelevant to student and/or learning goals.

Lesson 9.1 Activity
Coordinate Plane Treasure Hunt

1. Both players decide whether to use the Beginner or Advanced Treasure Hunt grid.

2. Both players mark on their graph paper where they will hide their treasure. The treasure is hidden under points on the coordinate plane. They can be placed horizontally or vertically anywhere on the grid. Each stash of treasure should be in a straight line. Circle each treasure stash.

Type of treasure	Number of locations	Size of location
Sapphire	1	5 points
Ruby	2	3 points
Gold	2	2 points
Diamond	3	1 point

Treasure Hunt Grid Example

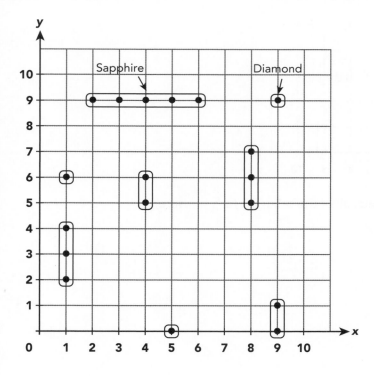

Lesson 9.1 Activity continued
Coordinate Plane Treasure Hunt

3. Players take turns asking each other to DIG at a coordinate pair. If the coordinates are SPOT ON, the player gets to guess again. If they are a MISS, the other player gets a turn.

A DIG is SPOT ON if it lands on a point with treasure marked on it. For example, if Player B calls out (4, 6), it is SPOT ON one of Player A's hidden treasure sites. A DIG is a MISS if it lands on a point with no treasure. If Player B calls out (9, 4), it is a MISS because Player A did not hide any treasure there.

Player A's Treasure Graph

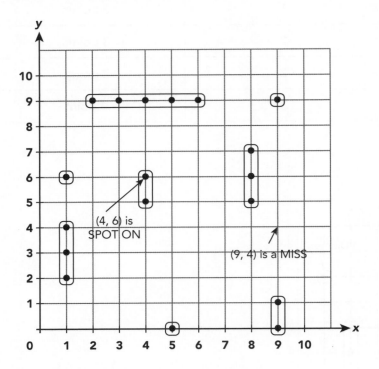

(4, 6) is SPOT ON

(9, 4) is a MISS

4. The game ends when one player finds all of the other player's treasure.

Lesson 9.1 Activity
Student Recording Sheet

1. Did you win or lose the Coordinate Plane Treasure Hunt?

2. Describe the strategy that you used.

Reflection

3. If you won the Treasure Hunt, how do you think was your strategy superior to the other player's strategy?

4. If you lost the Treasure Hunt, how can your strategy be improved?

Lesson 9.1 Activity continued
Materials

Treasure Hunt Grid (Beginner)

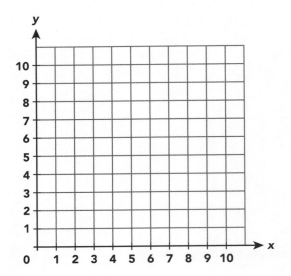

Treasure Hunt Grid (Advanced)

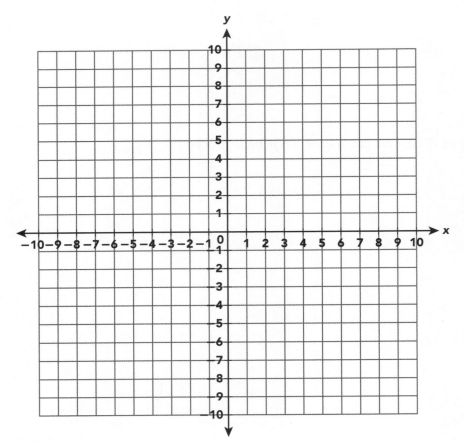

CHAPTER 9   The Coordinate Plane

Project: Graphing Rubber Band Data

Teacher's Guide

Common Core State Standard	6.NS.8 . . . [Graph] points in all four quadrants of the coordinate plane . . . .
Objective	Design and complete an experiment to investigate the effect of weight on a rubber band.
Materials	• Scissors • Graph paper • Modeling clay • Measuring tape or meter stick • Calculator (optional) • Scale (for use by the whole class) • At least two different types of rubber bands (The rubber bands may be of different thicknesses.)
Time	20–30 min
Ability levels	Mixed
Prerequisite skill	Plot points on a coordinate plane.
Grouping	Students should work in a small group.
Assessment of students' learning	See Chapter 9 Project: Rubric.
Preparation	Test the modeling clay and the rubber bands before starting the project to make sure that the clay sticks to the rubber bands. If you do not have a scale that can be used during class, you can prepare three 25-gram lumps of clay for each group before starting the project. If you do not have a classroom set of scissors, cut the rubber bands before distributing them to the students. Test the weights on the rubber bands to make sure that the heaviest weight doesn't break or deform the bands. If necessary, use lighter or heavier weights. If students have trouble measuring the length of the extended rubber band, suggest that they tape its free end to the edge of a table, and let the weight hang below the edge of the table.

Chapter 9 Project
Rubric

Category	4	3	2	1
Mathematical concepts	Explanation shows complete understanding of the mathematical concepts used to solve the problem(s).	Explanation shows substantial understanding of the mathematical concepts used to solve the problem(s).	Explanation shows some understanding of the mathematical concepts needed to solve the problem(s).	Explanation shows very limited understanding of the underlying concepts needed to solve the problem(s) OR is not written.
Strategy/ Procedures	Uses an efficient and effective strategy to solve the problem(s).	Uses an effective strategy to solve the problem(s).	Uses an effective strategy to solve problems, but does not do it consistently.	Does not use an effective strategy to solve problems.
Working with others	Student was an engaged partner, listening to suggestions of others and working cooperatively throughout lesson.	Student was an engaged partner but had trouble listening to others and/or working cooperatively.	Student cooperated with others, but needed prompting to stay on task.	Student did not work effectively with others.
Presentation	Presentation is detailed and clear.	Presentation is clear.	Presentation is a little difficult to understand, but includes critical components.	Presentation is difficult to understand and is missing several components OR is not included.
Neatness and organization	The work is presented in a neat, clear, organized fashion that is easy to read.	The work is presented in a neat and organized fashion that is usually easy to read.	The work is presented in an organized fashion but may be hard to read at times.	The work appears sloppy and unorganized. It is hard to know what information goes together.
Explanation	Explanation is detailed and clear.	Explanation is clear.	Explanation is a little difficult to understand, but includes critical components.	Explanation is difficult to understand and is missing several components OR is not included.

Chapter 9 Project
Graphing Rubber Band Data

In this project, you will measure the length of different types of rubber bands when they hold different masses.

Materials:
- Modeling clay
- Different types of rubber bands
- Measuring tape or meter stick
- Graph paper
- Calculator (optional)
- Scale (for use by the whole class)

1. Follow these steps with each of your rubber bands.
   Step 1 Cut the rubber band and lay it in a straight line without stretching it.

   Step 2 Attach a 25-gram lump of clay to one end of the rubber band.

   Step 3 Measure the remaining length of rubber band, again without stretching it. This is called the *initial length* of the rubber band.

   Step 4 Pick up the other end of the rubber band so that the clay is lifted off the table.

   Step 5 Measure the length of the stretched rubber band and record it. This is called the *extended length* of the rubber band.

   Step 6 Mold another 25-gram lump of clay onto the first piece of clay, so that the total weight of the clay is 50 grams. Make sure you do not change the initial length of the rubber band. Repeat Steps 4 and 5 with the new weight.

   Step 7 Add another 25-gram lump of clay to the end of the rubber band, so that the total weight of the clay is 75 grams. Repeat Steps 4 and 5 with the new weight.

2. Make a graph of your data. Use the x-axis for the mass of the clay and the y-axis for the extended length of the rubber band.

3. Use your graph to answer the questions on the Student Recording Sheet.

4. Prepare a simple presentation to share in class. Include a diagram of your experiment, your data and graphs, and your conclusions.

Chapter 9 Project
Student Recording Sheet

1. Describe how you carried out the experiment. Include the steps that you followed and a sketch of your setup.

2. Record your data in the tables.

Rubber band 1	
Mass	Length
0	

Rubber band 2	
Mass	Length
0	

3. Plot your data on graph paper. Put the mass of clay on the x-axis and the length of rubber band on the y-axis.

4. What type of graph did you draw for each rubber band?

5. How are the graphs for each rubber band different? How are they alike?

6. Use the data from one of your rubber bands. Subtract the initial length from each of the extended lengths to find the adjusted length. Then find the ratio $\frac{\text{adjusted length}}{\text{mass}}$ for each mass. Record your results in the table.

Mass	Adjusted length (Extended length − Initial length)	$\frac{\text{adjusted length}}{\text{mass}}$

What do you notice about the ratios in the third column of your table?

7. Why do you think some rubber bands stretched longer than others?

Area of Polygons

Lessons 10.1–10.3 Activity: Area of Triangles, Parallelograms, Trapezoids, and Other Polygons

Teacher's Guide

Type of activity	Hands-on activity and game
Objective	Reinforce the skill of solving problems involving areas of triangles, parallelograms, trapezoids, and other polygons.
Materials	Polygon cards on pages 115–118: • 10 triangle cards • 5 parallelogram cards • 6 trapezoid cards • 3 other polygon cards
Time	20–30 min
Ability level	Mixed
Prerequisite skills	Find the area of a triangle, parallelogram, trapezoid, and other polygons.
Grouping	Students should work with a partner.
Assessment of students' learning	See Lessons 10.1–10.3 Activity: Rubric.
Preparation	Make one set of polygon cards per group.

Lessons 10.1–10.3 Activity Rubric

Category	4	3	2	1
Mathematical concepts	Student shows complete understanding of the mathematical concepts used to solve the problem(s).	Student shows substantial understanding of the mathematical concepts used to solve the problem(s).	Student shows some understanding of the mathematical concepts needed to solve the problem(s).	Student shows very limited understanding of the underlying concepts needed to solve the problem(s).
Reflection	The reflections show significant thought and effort. The learning experience being reflected upon is relevant and meaningful to student and learning goals.	The reflections show considerable thought and effort. Student makes attempts to demonstrate relevance, but the relevance to learning goals is unclear.	The reflections show some thought and effort. Some sections of the reflection are irrelevant to student and/or learning goals.	The reflection is superficial. Most of the reflection is irrelevant to student and/or learning goals.

Lessons 10.1–10.3 Activity
Area of Triangles, Parallelograms, Trapezoids, and Other Polygons

Materials:
- Polygon cards

Step 1 Shuffle the cards and place them in the center of the table, face down.

Step 2 Player 1 draws one card and shows it to Player 2.

Step 3 If a triangle, parallelogram, or trapezoid card is drawn, Player 2 has 30 seconds to solve the problem correctly. If it is a hexagon or a pentagon card, Player 2 has 2 minutes to solve it.

Step 4 Player 1 checks Player 2's work and answer. If Player 2 has solved it correctly, he or she gets to keep the card. If the answer is wrong, place the card at the bottom of the deck.

Step 5 Record your results on the Student Recording Sheet.

Step 6 Switch roles and repeat Steps 2 to 5.

Step 7 The player with the most cards after 20 minutes of play wins.

Lessons 10.1–10.3 Activity
Student Recording Sheet

Score Card

Round	Problem I was asked to solve	My answer	Correct answer	Correct?
Example	Triangle, base = 5 cm, height = 2 cm, area = ?	5 cm^2	5 cm^2	Yes
1				
2				
3				
4				
5				
6				
7				
8				
9				
10				
11				
12				
13				
14				
15				

Reflection

Describe what you learned from this activity. What type of problem did you find easiest? Which were more difficult? Did the time limits affect your work?

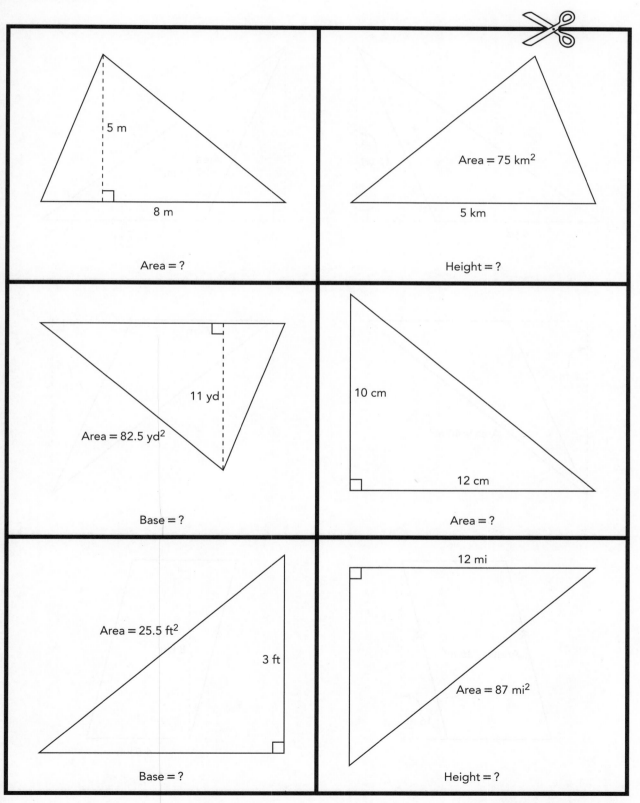

Area = ?

Height = ?

Base = ?

Area = ?

Base = ?

Height = ?

Lessons 10.1–10.3 Activity continued
Materials

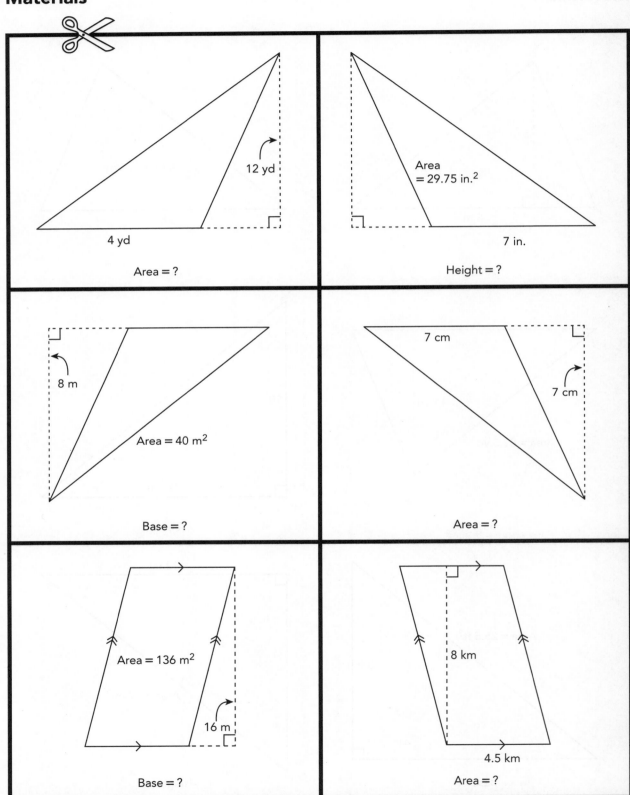

12 yd

4 yd

Area = ?

Area = 29.75 in.²

7 in.

Height = ?

---

8 m

Area = 40 m²

Base = ?

---

7 cm

7 cm

Area = ?

Area = 136 m²

16 m

Base = ?

---

8 km

4.5 km

Area = ?

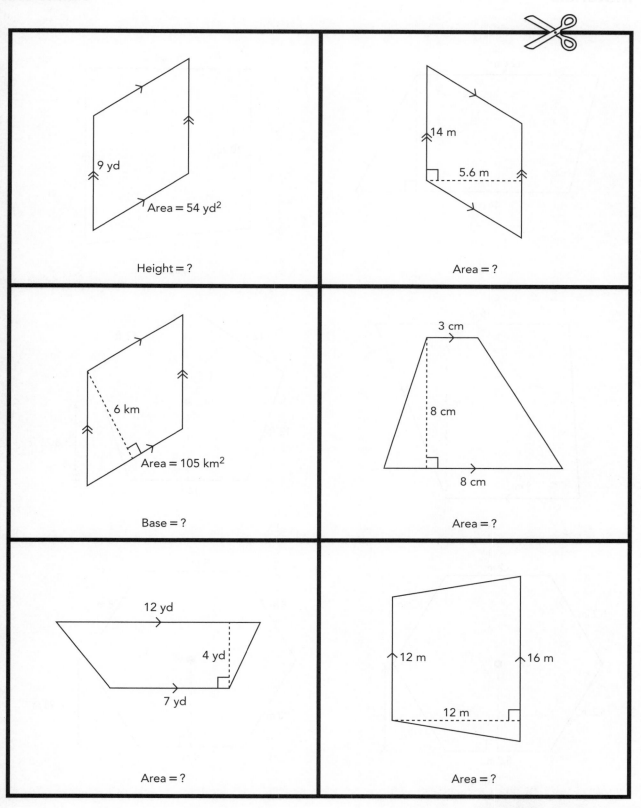

Height = ?

Area = ?

Base = ?

Area = ?

Area = ?

Area = ?

Lessons 10.1–10.3 Activity continued
Materials

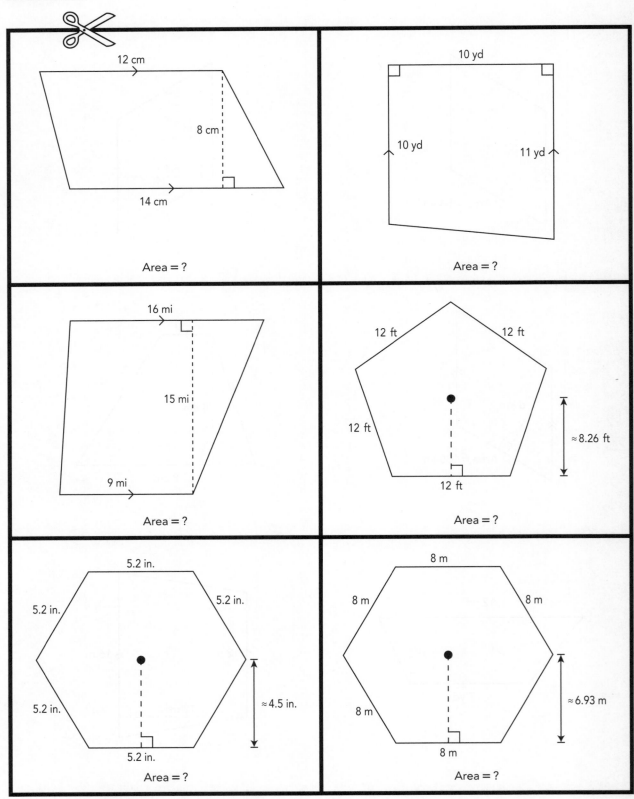

CHAPTER 10 Area of Polygons

Project: Area Puzzle

Teacher's Guide

Common Core State Standard	6.G.1 Find the area of right triangles, other triangles, special quadrilaterals, and polygons by composing into rectangles . . . .
Objective	Find the area of a composite figure.
Materials	• Copy of the four polygons on page 121 • Scissors • Ruler • Glue or tape • Calculator (optional)
Time	20–30 min
Ability levels	Mixed
Prerequisite skills	Find the area of a square, triangle, parallelogram, trapezoid, and other polygons.
Grouping	Students should work with a partner or in a small group.
Assessment of students' learning	See Chapter 10 Project: Rubric.
Preparation	In this project, minimal information is intentionally given to the students to encourage them to "think out of the box." Give students at least 10 minutes to work before giving hints about forming a bigger shape out of the four polygons. Avoid giving students clues about what shape to make. The polygons are drawn to scale, so it is possible for students to trace, cut out, and put the polygons together to form a triangle or a square, measure the sides, and find the area. Photocopying the polygons may result in slight discrepancies in measurements, so ensure that the cutouts will actually form an equilateral triangle or a square. For this reason, solutions may also vary slightly.

Chapter 10 Project
Rubric

Category	4	3	2	1
Mathematical concepts	Explanation shows complete understanding of the mathematical concepts used to solve the problem(s).	Explanation shows substantial understanding of the mathematical concepts used to solve the problem(s).	Explanation shows some understanding of the mathematical concepts needed to solve the problem(s).	Explanation shows very limited understanding of the underlying concepts needed to solve the problem(s) OR is not written.
Mathematical reasoning	Uses complex and refined mathematical reasoning.	Uses effective mathematical reasoning.	Shows some evidence of mathematical reasoning.	Shows little evidence of mathematical reasoning.
Strategy/ Procedures	Typically uses an efficient and effective strategy to solve the problem(s).	Typically uses an effective strategy to solve the problem(s).	Sometimes uses an effective strategy to solve problems, but does not do it consistently.	Rarely uses an effective strategy to solve problems.
Working with others	Student was an engaged partner, listening to suggestions of others and working cooperatively throughout lesson.	Student was an engaged partner but had trouble listening to others and/or working cooperatively.	Student cooperated with others, but needed prompting to stay on task.	Student did not work effectively with others.
Presentation	Presentation of mathematical calculations is detailed and clear.	Presentation of mathematical calculations is clear.	Presentation of mathematical calculations is a little difficult to understand, but includes critical components.	Presentation of mathematical calculations is difficult to understand and is missing several components OR is not included.
Explanation	Explanation is detailed and clear.	Explanation is clear.	Explanation is a little difficult to understand, but includes critical components.	Explanation is difficult to understand and is missing several components OR is not included.

Chapter 10 Project
Area Puzzle

Materials: Scissors, ruler, glue

1. The polygons below are drawn to scale. Your job is to find the total area of the polygons, to the nearest square centimeter.

2. Discuss with your group how to solve the problem.

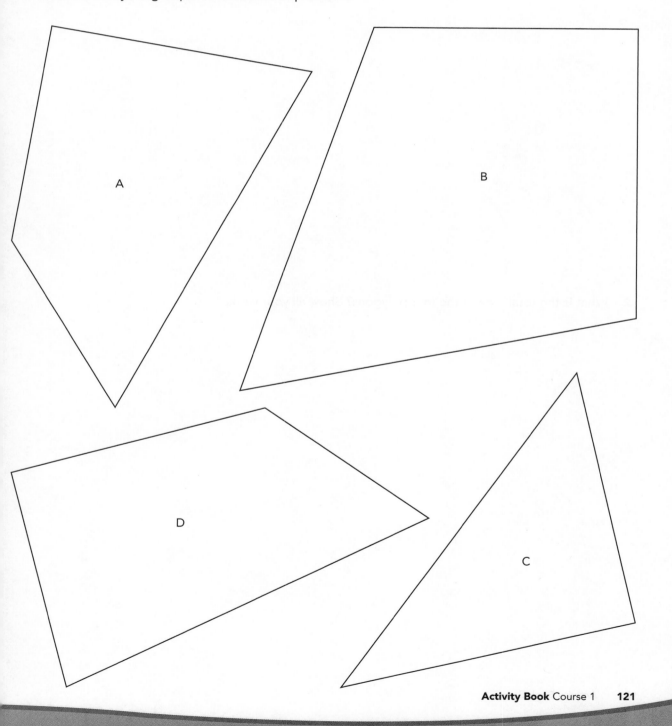

Chapter 10 Project
Student Recording Sheet

1. Describe how your group solved the problem. Show any sketches that you used.

2. What is the total area of the four polygons? Show all your work.

Circumference and Area of a Circle

Lesson 11.2 Activity: Area of a Circle

Teacher's Guide

Type of activity	Foundational activity for students needing extra help Hands-on activity Calculator activity
Objective	Reinforce understanding of the area of a circle.
Materials	• Small circular objects, such as cans or cups • Scissors • Glue • String about 12 inches long • Ruler • Calculator
Time	20–30 min
Ability levels	Mixed
Prerequisite skills	Identify and measure the diameter, circumference, and area of a circle.
Grouping	Students should work alone or with a partner.
Assessment of students' learning	See Lesson 11.2 Activity: Rubric.

Lesson 11.2 Activity
Rubric

Category	4	3	2	1
Mathematical concepts	Explanation shows complete understanding of the mathematical concepts used to solve the problem(s).	Explanation shows substantial understanding of the mathematical concepts used to solve the problem(s).	Explanation shows some understanding of the mathematical concepts needed to solve the problem(s).	Explanation shows very limited understanding of the underlying concepts needed to solve the problem(s) OR is not written.
Mathematical reasoning	Uses complex and refined mathematical reasoning.	Uses effective mathematical reasoning.	Shows some evidence of mathematical reasoning.	Shows little evidence of mathematical reasoning.
Working with others	Student was an engaged partner, listening to suggestions of others and working cooperatively throughout lesson.	Student was an engaged partner but had trouble listening to others and/or working cooperatively.	Student cooperated with others, but needed prompting to stay on task.	Student did not work effectively with others.
Checking	The work is checked by two classmates and all appropriate corrections are made.	The work is checked by one classmate and all appropriate corrections are made.	Work is checked by one classmate but some corrections are not made.	Work is not checked by classmate OR no corrections are made based on feedback.
Neatness and organization	The work is presented in a neat, clear, organized fashion that is easy to read.	The work is presented in a neat and organized fashion that is usually easy to read.	The work is presented in an organized fashion but may be hard to read at times.	The work appears sloppy and unorganized. It is hard to know what information goes together.
Explanation	Explanation is detailed and clear.	Explanation is clear.	Explanation is a little difficult to understand, but includes critical components.	Explanation is difficult to understand and is missing several components OR is not included.

Lesson 11.2 Activity
Area of a Circle

Materials:
- String
- Ruler
- Scissors
- Glue
- Calculator

1. Use a circular object such as a small can or a cup. Measure its diameter and circumference, using the ruler and string.

2. Trace the circumference of the object on a sheet of paper with a pencil. Make two copies and cut them out.

3. On one circle, draw 8 diameters that divide the circle into 16 equal pieces. Cut them out. Using the diagrams on page 137 of Chapter 11 in your textbook as a guide, make a polygon from the 16 pieces of the circle. Glue the pieces on another piece of paper and find the area of the polygon you made. Write your results on the Student Recording Sheet.

4. Use the other cutout. Find its area and circumference using the formulas that you learned in class. Write your results on the Student Recording Sheet.

5. Answer the questions on the Student Recording Sheet.

Name: _____   Date: _____

Lesson 11.2 Activity
Student Recording Sheet

The object I selected: _____

Measurements that I made

Object	Diameter	Circumference

Circumference and area that I found in Step 3

Diameter of object	Circumference using 3.14 for π	Circumference using $\frac{22}{7}$ for π	Area using 3.14 for π	Area using $\frac{22}{7}$ for π

Circumference and area that I found in Step 4

Diameter of object	Circumference using 3.14 for π	Circumference using $\frac{22}{7}$ for π	Area using 3.14 for π	Area using $\frac{22}{7}$ for π

1. Compare the area that you found in Step 3 with the area you found in Step 4. Did you get the same area for the two circles?

2. If the areas are not equal, what could have caused the difference between them?

3. In your opinion, which is the more accurate way of finding the circumference of a circle, using the string or using the formula? Explain.

4. In your opinion, which is the more accurate way of finding the area of a circle, the method used in Step 3, or the formula? Explain.

CHAPTER 11 Circumference and Area of a Circle

Project: A Triangle Inscribed in a Semicircle

Teacher's Guide

Common Core	
Common Core State Standard	7.G.4 Solve problems involving the diameter and radius of a circle.
Objective	Draw conclusions about the angles of a triangle inscribed in a semicircle.
Materials	*For each group:* • Protractor • Compass • Ruler or straightedge
Time	20–30 min
Ability levels	Mixed
Prerequisite skills	Draw a circle with a compass. Measure an angle with a protractor.
Grouping	Students should work with a partner or in a small group.
Assessment of students' learning	See Chapter 11 Project: Rubric.

Chapter 11 Project
Rubric

Category	4	3	2	1
Mathematical concepts	Explanation shows complete understanding of the mathematical concepts used to solve the problem(s).	Explanation shows substantial understanding of the mathematical concepts used to solve the problem(s).	Explanation shows some understanding of the mathematical concepts needed to solve the problem(s).	Explanation shows very limited understanding of the underlying concepts needed to solve the problem(s) OR is not written.
Mathematical reasoning	Uses complex and refined mathematical reasoning.	Uses effective mathematical reasoning.	Shows some evidence of mathematical reasoning.	Shows little evidence of mathematical reasoning.
Explanation	Explanation is detailed and clear.	Explanation is clear.	Explanation is a little difficult to understand, but includes critical components.	Explanation is difficult to understand and is missing several components OR is not included.
Working with others	Student was an engaged partner, listening to suggestions of others and working cooperatively throughout lesson.	Student was an engaged partner but had trouble listening to others and/or working cooperatively.	Student cooperated with others, but needed prompting to stay on task.	Student did not work effectively with others.

Chapter 11 Project
A Triangle Inscribed in a Semicircle

Peter notices that if points *A*, *B*, and *C* are points on a circle and $\overline{AC}$ is a diameter of the circle, then $\angle ABC$ is a right angle. Susan thinks that it is a coincidence and not true for all cases. What do you think?

Step 1 Use a compass to draw a circle. Draw two points that are the endpoints of a diameter of the circle, and a third point anywhere on the circle. Use a ruler or straightedge to connect the points to make a triangle.

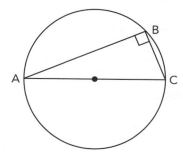

Step 2 Use a protractor to measure the angles of the triangle. Record your results in the table on the Student Recording Sheet.

Step 3 Repeat Steps 1 and 2 for at least three more circles.

Step 4 Look at the results for your triangles. Do you think that a triangle inscribed in a semicircle is always a right triangle?

Chapter 11 Project
Student Recording Sheet

1. Record the measures of the angles of your triangles in the table.

Triangle	m∠A	m∠B	m∠C

2. Describe any patterns you see in the table. Make a conclusion about a triangle that is inscribed in a semicircle.

Surface Area and Volume of Solids

Lesson 12.3 Activity: Volume of Prisms

Teacher's Guide

Type of activity	Foundational activity for students needing extra help Hands-on activity
Objective	Reinforce the skill of finding the volume of a prism.
Materials	• Calculator (optional; to be used if students have difficulty with calculations) • 3 identical sheets of paper • Tape • Scissors • Ruler
Time	20–30 min
Ability levels	Mixed
Prerequisite skill	Find the volume of rectangular and triangular prisms.
Grouping	Students should work with a partner.
Assessment of students' learning	See Lesson 12.3 Activity: Rubric.
Preparation	In this activity, students will find the volume formed by folding pieces of paper of the same size in different ways. If time permits, consider extending the activity by asking students to find the surface area of the solids they formed using the three methods of folding.

Lesson 12.3 Activity
Rubric

Category	4	3	2	1
Mathematical concepts	Explanation shows complete understanding of the mathematical concepts used to solve the problem(s).	Explanation shows substantial understanding of the mathematical concepts used to solve the problem(s).	Explanation shows some understanding of the mathematical concepts needed to solve the problem(s).	Explanation shows very limited understanding of the underlying concepts needed to solve the problem(s) OR is not written.
Reflection	The reflections show tremendous thought and effort. The learning experience being reflected upon is relevant and meaningful to student and learning goals.	The reflections show considerable thought and effort. Student makes attempts to demonstrate relevance, but the relevance to learning goals is unclear.	The reflections show some thought and effort. Some sections of the reflection are irrelevant to student and/or learning goals.	The reflection is superficial. Most of the reflection is irrelevant to student and/or learning goals.

Lesson 12.3 Activity
Volume of Prisms

Materials:
* Three sheets of paper, all the same size

Hold the first sheet of paper lengthwise and fold it to form an open rectangular prism with a square base, as shown.

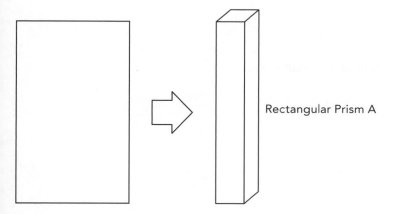

Rectangular Prism A

Hold the second sheet of paper crosswise and fold it to form a different rectangular prism with an open square base, as shown.

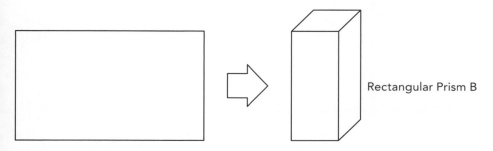

Rectangular Prism B

Fold the third sheet of paper to form a triangular prism with an open base, as shown.

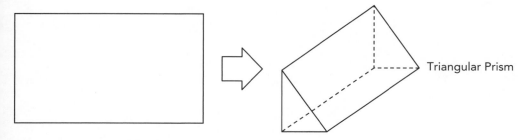

Triangular Prism

Your prisms should have no overlapping sides.

Your job is to decide which method of folding results in the prism with the greatest volume.

Lesson 12.3 Activity
Student Recording Sheet

1. Find the volume of rectangular prism A. Show all your work.

2. Find the volume of rectangular prism B. Show all your work.

3. Find the volume of the triangular prism. Show all your work.

4. The method that gives the greatest volume is _____.

Reflection

Describe what you discovered in this activity. Were your results surprising to you?

CHAPTER 12 Surface Area and Volume of Solids

Project: Surface Area and Volume of Real-Life Objects

Teacher's Guide

Common Core State Standard	7.G.6 Solve real-world problems involving surface areas and volume of solids, including composite solids.
Objective	Find the surface area and volume of a composite figure.
Materials	• Cabinet, shelving unit, or bookcase, or a sketch of one, including measurements • Tape measure • Calculator
Time	20–30 min
Ability levels	Mixed
Prerequisite skills	Find the areas of squares and rectangles. Find the volumes of cubes and prisms.
Grouping	Students should work with a partner or in small groups.
Assessment of students' learning	See Chapter 12 Project: Rubric.
Preparation	If students have difficulty starting the solution, suggest they use shapes such as squares and rectangles to approximate the different parts of the cabinet. If a cabinet is not available, you may wish to use a shelf or any other storage unit or container. If none of these are available, a picture can be used, but be sure to include its dimensions, including the thickness of the material, and the length, width, and height of the inside of the container.

Chapter 12 Project
Rubric

Category	4	3	2	1
Mathematical concepts	Explanation shows complete understanding of the mathematical concepts used to solve the problem(s).	Explanation shows substantial understanding of the mathematical concepts used to solve the problem(s).	Explanation shows some understanding of the mathematical concepts needed to solve the problem(s).	Explanation shows very limited understanding of the underlying concepts needed to solve the problem(s) OR is not written.
Mathematical reasoning	Uses complex and refined mathematical reasoning.	Uses effective mathematical reasoning.	Shows some evidence of mathematical reasoning.	Shows little evidence of mathematical reasoning.
Strategy/ Procedures	Uses an efficient and effective strategy to solve the problem(s).	Uses an effective strategy to solve the problem(s).	Uses an effective strategy to solve the problem(s), but does not do it consistently.	Does not use an effective strategy to solve the problem(s).
Working with others	Student was an engaged partner, listening to suggestions of others and working cooperatively throughout the lesson.	Student was an engaged partner but had trouble listening to others and/or working cooperatively.	Student cooperated with others, but needed prompting to stay on task.	Student did not work effectively with others.
Explanation	Explanation is detailed and clear.	Explanation is clear.	Explanation is a little difficult to understand, but includes critical components.	Explanation is difficult to understand and is missing several components OR is not included.

Chapter 12 Project
Surface Area and Volume of Real-Life Objects

1. Your teacher will show your group a piece of furniture to decorate. It will be used to store art materials. The art materials will be kept in containers that are 20 cm by 12 cm by 10 cm. As the piece of furniture is old, your task is to wrap it inside and out using some decorative paper.

2. Find a way to estimate how much wrapping paper is needed to decorate the piece of furniture.

3. Find the maximum number of containers that can be stored in the piece of furniture.

4. Summarize your group's results and prepare a simple presentation to share in class. Include any diagrams or sketches you made, your calculations, and your conclusions.

Chapter 12 Project
Student Recording Sheet

1. Describe the approach that your group took to estimate the amount of decorative paper required to wrap the piece of furniture inside and out. Show all your work.

2. Describe how you estimated the maximum number of containers that can fit inside the piece of furniture. Show all your work.

Introduction to Statistics

Lesson 13.1 Activity: Collecting and Tabulating Data

Teacher's Guide

Type of activity	Foundational activity for students needing extra help Calculator activity
Objective	Reinforce the skill of collecting, organizing, and tabulating data.
Materials	Paper and pencil
Time	20–30 min
Ability levels	Mixed
Prerequisite skills	Write survey questions. Organize data in a tally chart.
Grouping	Students should work with a partner.
Assessment of students' learning	See Lesson 13.1 Activity: Rubric.
Preparation	In this activity, students will choose an interesting survey topic, write a simple question about it, present the results in an organized manner, and draw conclusions based on their findings. Encourage students to develop original ideas for their questions.

Lesson 13.1 Activity Rubric

Category	4	3	2	1
Mathematical concepts	Explanation shows complete understanding of the mathematical concepts used to solve the problem(s).	Explanation shows substantial understanding of the mathematical concepts used to solve the problem(s).	Explanation shows some understanding of the mathematical concepts needed to solve the problem(s).	Explanation shows very limited understanding of the underlying concepts needed to solve the problem(s) OR is not written.
Working with others	Student was an engaged partner, listening to suggestions of others and working cooperatively throughout the lesson.	Student was an engaged partner but had trouble listening to others and/or working cooperatively.	Student cooperated with others, but needed prompting to stay on task.	Student did not work effectively with others.

Lesson 13.1 Activity
Collecting and Tabulating Data

Choose an interesting survey question that you can use to collect data from your classmates quickly. For example, you might want to ask each classmate what his or her dream profession is, or the countries he or she would like to visit. The topic can be anything that you would like to find out about your classmates.

The answers to your question should include several different options. For example, if you want to find out what your classmates' dream professions are, you may have them select from a list of six different jobs. You may choose to group some answers in a general category, such as "Artist" (for musicians, actors, dancers, and painters), or include "Other" among your options if there are many possible answers to your question.

Record the results of your survey in the tally chart on the Student Recording Sheet.

Write three conclusions based on the data you have collected and share them in class.

Lesson 13.1 Activity
Student Recording Sheet

1. Write your survey question(s) below.

2. Use this tally chart to record the data that you have collected.

Answers	Tally	Frequency

3. Write three conclusions, based on your results.

CHAPTER 13 Introduction to Statistics

Project: Using Statistics to Find Solutions to Real-Life Problems

Teacher's Guide

Common Core State Standard	6.SP.1 Recognize a statistical question as one that anticipates variability in the data related to the question and accounts for it in the answers . . . 6.SP.4 Display numerical data in plots on a number line, including dot plots, histograms . . . .
Objective	Apply statistical knowledge to find solutions to real-life problems.
Materials	Paper and pencil
Ability levels	Mixed
Prerequisite skills	Write statistical questions. Plan the best way to collect data related to a statistical question and the best data display (tally chart, dot plot, or histogram) to organize the results.
Time	30 min
Grouping	Students should work in small groups.
Assessment of students' learning	See Chapter 13 Project: Rubric.
Preparation	This project is intended to assess the students' ability to develop interesting statistical questions on their own. Encourage students to use original ideas.

Chapter 13 Project
Rubric

Category	4	3	2	1
Mathematical concepts	Explanation shows complete understanding of the mathematical concepts used to solve the problem(s).	Explanation shows substantial understanding of the mathematical concepts used to solve the problem(s).	Explanation shows some understanding of the mathematical concepts needed to solve the problem(s).	Explanation shows very limited understanding of the underlying concepts needed to solve the problem(s) OR is not written.
Mathematical reasoning	Uses complex and refined mathematical reasoning.	Uses effective mathematical reasoning.	Shows some evidence of mathematical reasoning.	Shows little evidence of mathematical reasoning.
Strategy/ Procedures	Uses an efficient and effective strategy to solve the problem(s).	Uses an effective strategy to solve the problem(s).	Uses an effective strategy to solve the problem(s), but does not do it consistently.	Does not use an effective strategy to solve the problem(s).
Working with others	Student was an engaged partner, listening to suggestions of others and working cooperatively throughout the lesson.	Student was an engaged partner but had trouble listening to others and/or working cooperatively.	Student cooperated with others, but needed prompting to stay on task.	Student did not work effectively with others.
Explanation	Explanation is detailed and clear.	Explanation is clear.	Explanation is a little difficult to understand, but includes critical components.	Explanation is difficult to understand and is missing several components OR is not included.

Chapter 13 Project
Using Statistics to Find Solutions to Real-Life Problems

Choose an interesting and useful topic and write a statistical question related to it. A statistical question is one whose answers can be used as pieces of data. For example, "How many hours do the students in our class exercise every week?"

Write the question so that you can use your data to make a suggestion that benefits your class or school. In other words, your statistical question must have a purpose. The example given above could be used to recommend a certain amount of weekly exercise time for your class.

On the Student Recording Sheet, describe how you would collect data to answer your question: by observation, interviews, or using a questionnaire. Be sure to write the specific questions for an interview or in your questionnaire, or to specify exactly what you will observe if you collect data by observation.

Choose the best form of display for your data: a tally chart, dot plot, or histogram. On the recording sheet, predict the results, and write your recommendation(s) based on it.

Chapter 13 Project
Student Recording Sheet

Statistical question	
Purpose	
How to collect data	
How to display data	
Predicted results	
Recommendations	

Measures of Central Tendency

14

Lesson 14.1 Activity: Mean

Teacher's Guide

Type of activity	Foundational activity for students needing extra help Calculator activity
Objective	Reinforce the skill of finding the mean of a set of data.
Material	Calculator
Time	20 min
Ability levels	Mixed
Prerequisite skills	Draw a tally chart to organize data. Find the average of a data set.
Grouping	Students should work with a partner.
Assessment of students' learning	See Lesson 14.1 Activity: Rubric.

Lesson 14.1 Activity
Rubric

Category	4	3	2	1
Mathematical concepts	Explanation shows complete understanding of the mathematical concepts used to solve the problem(s).	Explanation shows substantial understanding of the mathematical concepts used to solve the problem(s).	Explanation shows some understanding of the mathematical concepts needed to solve the problem(s).	Explanation shows very limited understanding of the underlying concepts needed to solve the problem(s) OR is not written.
Presentation	Presentation of mathematical calculations is detailed and clear.	Presentation of mathematical calculations is clear.	Presentation of mathematical calculations is a little difficult to understand, but includes critical components.	Presentation of mathematical calculations is difficult to understand and is missing several components OR is not included.
Working with others	Student was an engaged partner, listening to suggestions of others and working cooperatively throughout the lesson.	Student was an engaged partner but had trouble listening to others and/or working cooperatively.	Student cooperated with others, but needed prompting to stay on task.	Student did not work effectively with others.

Lesson 14.1 Activity
Mean

In this activity, you will count the number of times the digits 0 to 9 appear in the numbers 1 to 99. Use a data table or chart to help organize your data.

Then, you will find, on average, how many times an odd or even digit appears in the numbers from 1 to 99.

Use the questions on the Student Recording Sheet to summarize your results and prepare to share them with the class.

Lesson 14.1 Activity
Student Recording Sheet

1. Write the numbers from 1 to 99 in a table or an organized list.

2. Make a table that shows the total number of occurrences of each digit in the numbers 1 to 99. For example, for the number 35, add one tally to 3 and one tally to 5.

3. Find the mean occurrence for all the odd digits and all the even digits.

CHAPTER 14   Measures of Central Tendency

Project: Number Cube Data

Teacher's Guide

Common Core	
Common Core State Standard	6.SP.3 Recognize that a measure of center for a numerical data set summarizes all of its values with a single number . . . .
Objective	Apply the concepts of mean, median, and mode to determine whether or not a number cube is fair.
Materials	*For each group:* • One number cube, numbered 1 to 6 • Calculator
Time	20–30 min
Ability levels	Mixed
Prerequisite skills	Find the mean, the median, and the mode of a data set.
Grouping	Students should work in a small group.
Assessment of students' learning	See Chapter 14 Project: Rubric.

Chapter 14 Project
Rubric

Category	4	3	2	1
Mathematical concepts	Explanation shows complete understanding of the mathematical concepts used to solve the problem(s).	Explanation shows substantial understanding of the mathematical concepts used to solve the problem(s).	Explanation shows some understanding of the mathematical concepts needed to solve the problem(s).	Explanation shows very limited understanding of the underlying concepts needed to solve the problem(s) OR is not written.
Mathematical reasoning	Uses complex and refined mathematical reasoning.	Uses effective mathematical reasoning.	Shows some evidence of mathematical reasoning.	Shows little evidence of mathematical reasoning.
Strategy/ Procedures	Uses an efficient and effective strategy to solve the problem(s).	Uses an effective strategy to solve the problem(s).	Uses an effective strategy to solve the problem(s), but does not do it consistently.	Does not use an effective strategy to solve the problem(s).
Working with others	Student was an engaged partner, listening to suggestions of others and working cooperatively throughout the lesson.	Student was an engaged partner but had trouble listening to others and/or working cooperatively.	Student cooperated with others, but needed prompting to stay on task.	Student did not work effectively with others.
Explanation	Explanation is detailed and clear.	Explanation is clear.	Explanation is a little difficult to understand, but includes critical components.	Explanation is difficult to understand and is missing several components OR is not included.

Chapter 14 Project
Number Cube Data

Your group will use a number cube, numbered 1 to 6. In this project, you will decide if the number cube is *fair*, based on the data you collect and the three measures of central tendency. A number cube is called **fair** if each side has an equal chance of turning up.

Roll the number cube several times and find the following:

1. The mean of the values you rolled. For example, if you roll the number cube twice and you get 4 and 6, then the mean value is $(4 + 6) \div 2 = 5$.

2. The median value. For example, if you roll the number cube 5 times and you arrange the numbers you get from least to greatest, the middle value (the third number) is the median of the data set.

3. The mode. This is the number that you rolled most frequently.

Decide whether the number cube is fair, based on the data you collected. Which of the measures of central tendency can help you decide if the number cube is fair?

Use the questions on the Student Recording Sheet to summarize your results and prepare to share them with the class.

Chapter 14 Project
Student Recording Sheet

1. Describe how your group plans to collect data. How many times will you roll the number cube? How will you keep track of your results?

2. Draw a table to record your data. Show all your work.

3. Find the mean, the median, and the mode of the data you collected.

4. Is the number cube *fair*, *not fair*, or *nearly fair*? Explain.

Solutions

Lesson 1.2 Activity (p. 4)

Answers will vary. Sample:

Prime number	7	11	13	17	29
Square of the prime number	49	121	169	289	841
Add 17	66	138	186	306	858
Divide by 12	5.5	11.5	15.5	25.5	71.5
Remainder	6	6	6	6	6

1. The remainders are all 6.

   Note for the teacher: If a remainder is not 6, the student has either made a computational error or chosen a number that is not prime.

2. Any prime number greater than 5 will give a remainder of 6 after completing the steps.

3. We can use this process to check whether a number is prime or not.

Chapter 1 Project (p. 8)

1. Answers may vary. Sample:
   $25 = 2 + 23$
   $36 = 13 + 23$
   $49 = 2 + 47$
   $64 = 17 + 47$
   $81 = 2 + 79$
   $100 = 3 + 97$
   $121 = $ not possible
   $144 = 47 + 97$
   $169 = 2 + 167$
   $196 = 29 + 167$
   $225 = 2 + 223$

2. The square of an even number is even. The square of an odd number is odd.

3. The sum of two even numbers is even, and the sum of two odd numbers is even. The sum of one odd number and one even number is an odd number.

4. One square, 121, which is an odd number, cannot be expressed as a sum of two prime numbers. To write 121 as a sum, one addend must be an odd number and the other an even number. Since 2 is the only even prime number, the odd number must be 119, because $121 = 2 + 119$. However, 119 is not a prime number. So 121 cannot be written as the sum of two prime numbers.

Lesson 2.1 Activity (p. 12)

Reflections will vary.

Chapter 2 Project (p. 16)

1.

2.

3.

With opposites (points graphed in gray are opposites):

1.

2.
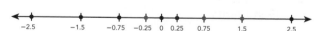

3.

Questions

4. Answers may vary. Sample: A point and its opposite are the same distance from 0 on the number line; for some of the points, the opposite was already graphed.

5. The opposite of n is $-n$. The opposite of $-n$ is $-(-n)$, or n.

6. Answers may vary. Sample: To graph the opposite of -8, count 8 units from 0 in the opposite direction, and you end up at 8.

Lesson 3.1 Activity (p. 20)

Answers will vary.

Lessons 3.2–3.3 Activity (p. 30)

1. a) 45 pounds of clay
   $16.50 \div 50 = \$0.33$ for 1 lb
   $0.33 \times 45 = \$14.85$ for 45 lb
   b) 32 ounces of ceramic glaze
   $3.08 \div 4 = \$0.77$ for 1 oz
   $0.77 \times 32 = \$24.64$ for 32 oz
   c) 150 sheets of paper
   $28.75 \div 125 = \$0.23$ for 1 sheet
   $0.23 \times 150 = \$34.50$ for 150 sheets
   d) 20 colors of watercolor paint
   $5.22 \div 18 = \$0.29$ for 1 color
   $0.29 \times 20 = \$5.80$ for 20 colors

2. a) Paintbrushes
   $33.95 \div 5 = \$6.79$ for
   1 paintbrush
   $\$100 \div 6.79 \approx 14.7$
   14 paintbrushes
   b) Drawing pencils
   $8.52 \div 12 = \$.71$ for
   1 drawing pencil
   $\$100 \div 0.71 \approx 140.8$
   140 drawing pencils

3. $48 \div 2.5 = 19.2$
   19 students

4. $45 - 2.25 = 42.75$ lb
   $42.75 \div 2.25 = 19$
   19 more flowerpots

Chapter 3 Project (p. 34)

1. List all the possible combinations of length and width and find the area for each combination.

Since the total length of fencing is 66 yards, which is equal to the perimeter of the fence, the sum of the length and width should be $66 \div 2 = 33$ yards.

And since each fence panel is $\frac{3}{4}$ yard long, the measurement of each length and width should be divisible by $\frac{3}{4}$.

Length (yd)	Width (yd)	Area (yd²)	Biggest?
15	18	270	
$15\frac{3}{4}$	$17\frac{1}{4}$	$271\frac{11}{16}$	
$16\frac{1}{2}$	$16\frac{1}{2}$	$272\frac{1}{4}$	Yes
$17\frac{1}{4}$	$15\frac{3}{4}$	$271\frac{11}{16}$	
18	15	270	

2. From the table, you can see that the largest possible area is that of a square with sides measuring $16\frac{1}{2}$ yards by $16\frac{1}{2}$ yards. The area is $272\frac{1}{4}$ square yards. (Note: A square is a special type of rectangle.)

3. There will be $16\frac{1}{2} \div \frac{3}{4} = 22$ fence panels on each side of the square area.

Notes for the teacher: For any polygon with a given perimeter, an equilateral shape will enclose the greatest area. For four-sided figures, the square will have the maximum area. A circle, however, will have a greater area than any polygon that has the same perimeter as the circle's circumference. For example:

Shape	Perimeter	Area
Rectangle	32 yd	60 yd² (10 × 6)
Square	32 yd	64 yd² (8 × 8)
Circle	32 yd	81.5 yd² (diameter = 10.1818 yd)

Lesson 4.2 Activity (pp. 39–40)

Answers will vary.

Chapter 4 Project (pp. 44–46)

1.

2. The ratio of the length of the forearm to the length of the hand is about the golden ratio.

3. Length divided by width approximates the golden ratio.
$5 \div 3 = 1.66$

3 inches

5 inches

4. The 'shallow diagonals' of Pascal's triangle have sums equal to the Fibonacci numbers.

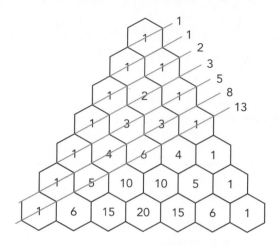

5. There are many golden ratios, but the three basic ones are $AD : AN$, $AN : AJ$, and $AJ : NJ$. Any segment congruent to the given segments can be substituted in these ratios to form more golden ratios. Other distances (as opposed to segments) that form a golden ratio are $AN : NL$ and $AD : DC$.

6. Answers will vary.

Lesson 5.2 Activity (p. 50)

1. Total area to be painted (square meters)

Room	Walls	Ceiling	Door	Window	Total area to be painted
1	4(6 × 3) = 72	6 × 6 = 36	1 × 2 = 2	3 × 2 = 6	72 + 36 − 2 − 6 = 100
2	2(8 × 3) + 2(6 × 3) = 84	8 × 6 = 48	1 × 2 = 2	3 × 2 = 6	84 + 48 − 2 − 6 = 124
3	2(9 × 3) + 2(6 × 3) = 90	9 × 6 = 54	1 × 2 = 2	3 × 2 = 6	90 + 54 − 2 − 6 = 136
4	2(9 × 3) + 2(6 × 3) = 90	9 × 6 = 54	1 × 2 = 2	3 × 2 = 6	90 + 54 − 2 − 6 = 136

(Continues on next page)

Room	Walls	Ceiling	Door	Window	Total area to be painted
5	4(6 × 3) = 72	6 × 6 = 36	1 × 2 = 2	3 × 2 = 6	72 + 36 − 2 − 6 = 100
6	2(8 × 3) + 2(6 × 3) = 84	8 × 6 = 48	1 × 2 = 2	3 × 2 = 6	84 + 48 − 2 − 6 = 124
				Total	720

2. Area each painter can paint in one day (square meters)

Painter	Speed × hours available	Total area (m²)
Junior painter	10 m²/h × 8 h	80
Senior painter	15 m²/h × 8 h	120

3. Costs for three painters to paint the six classrooms

Type of painters	Number of painters	Total area painted per day	How many days needed to paint the total area?
Junior painters	3	3 × 80 = 240	720 ÷ 240 = 3
Senior painters	3	3 × 120 = 360	720 ÷ 360 = 2

Type of painters	Cost per day	Total cost	Unit rate per square meter
Junior painters	3 × 140 = 420	3 × 420 = $1,260	1,260 ÷ 720 = $1.75
Senior painters	3 × 175 = 525	2 × 525 = $1,050	1,050 ÷ 720 ≈ $1.46

4. Answers will vary, but should include information about the daily rates of the painters.

Chapter 5 Project (p. 54)

1. Answers will vary. Students should include a brief description of the experiment and diagrams. Sample:
We marked 3 strips of paper towel. The marks were 2 centimeters from one end.

Mikalya held the marked end in the water and Jason timed it for 20 seconds.

We measured the colored part of each strip and wrote the result in the table.

The absorption rate is the length we measured, divided by the time, which is 20 seconds.

2. Answers will vary based on the data collected by the students.

3. Answers will vary based on the data collected by the students.

Lesson 6.2 Activity (p. 58)

Problem	Answer
$\frac{14}{25}$	56%
$\frac{16}{64}$	25%
$\frac{48}{75}$	64%
$\frac{27}{54}$	50%
$\frac{24}{96}$	25%
$\frac{9}{75}$	12%
$\frac{36}{75}$	48%
$\frac{36}{80}$	45%
$\frac{72}{96}$	75%
$\frac{34}{85}$	40%
0.12	12%
0.56	56%
0.63	63%
0.42	42%
9.8	980%
3	300%
5.0	500%
0.04	4%

Problem	Answer
0.7	70%
2.06	206%
55%	0.55
12%	0.12
78%	0.78
27%	0.27
91%	0.91
42%	0.42
36%	0.36
59%	0.59
35%	$\frac{7}{20}$
46%	$\frac{35}{50}$
76%	$\frac{19}{25}$
58%	$\frac{29}{50}$
82%	$\frac{41}{50}$
64%	$\frac{16}{25}$
92%	$\frac{23}{25}$
28%	$\frac{7}{25}$

Lesson 6.3 Activity (p. 66)

1.

Type of bean	Adzuki bean	Black bean	Black-eyed pea
Number of seeds used	50	42	12
Number of seeds germinated	35	29	12
Percentage of seeds germinated	70%	69%	100%

Type of bean	Soy bean	Red bean	Mung bean	Pinto bean
Number of seeds used	75	60	15	46
Number of seeds germinated	69	48	12	40
Percentage of seeds germinated	92%	80%	80%	87%

2. $300 - 50 - 42 - 12 - 75 - 60$
   $= 61$ seeds

3. Two possible answers:
   a) mung bean and pinto bean
      $= 15 + 46 = 61$ seeds
   b) kidney bean $= 61$ seeds

   However, since the club used 7 bean types, answer is mung bean and pinto bean.

4. adzuki bean and black bean

Chapter 6 Project (p. 70)

1. Answers vary.

2. Answers vary depending on the data collected by the students. Sample:

Coin	Flip 10 times (heads)	Flip 20 times (heads)	Flip 30 times (heads)
Penny	4 out of 10 (40%)	12 out of 20 (60%)	18 out of 30 (60%)
Nickel			
Dime			
Quarter			

   Note for the teacher: Have students estimate their findings to the nearest percent.

3. Answers vary depending on the data collected by the students.

4. Answers vary depending on the data collected by the students.

Lesson 7.1 Activity (p. 74)

1. Answers may vary. Accept any logical answers.

2. Write the algebraic rule for a number grid with starting variable x:

$2x + 4$	$x + 21$
$13 - 3x$	$17 - x$

3. Test your rule by circling the incorrect values and replacing them with the correct ones. Fill in the missing values for the incomplete grid.

Lesson 7.2 Activity (p. 78)

1. Answers will vary. Sample:
   We wrote a number for each letter of the alphabet, starting with 1:

   A B C D E F...
   1 2 3 4 5 6...

   We looked at the letters already given. F is 6, and it translated to U, which is 21. G is 7, and it translated to X, which is 24. We made a table and figured out a general rule:

In	Out
6	21
7	24
x	$3x + 3$

   We tested it with some more of the letters that were given.

Using 3x + 3 for the key, we completed the decoding wheel:

Original	A	B	C	D	E	F	G
Coded	**F**	**I**	**L**	**O**	**R**	U	X

Original	H	I	J	K	L	M	N
Coded	A	**D**	**G**	J	M	P	S

Original	O	P	Q	R	S	T	U
Coded	**V**	**Y**	**B**	**E**	H	**K**	**N**

Original	V	W	X	Y	Z
Coded	Q	T	W	**Z**	**C**

2. Answers will vary.

3. Answers will vary. Sample: We started translating the message to see if it made sense.

4. U M R R F K V S L R
   F L E E A T O N C E

   T R F E R O D H L V Q R E R O
   W E A R E D I S C O V E R E D

   FLEE AT ONCE WE ARE DISCOVERED

Chapter 7 Project (p. 82)

1.

Triangle	1	2	3	4	5	6	7	8
Number of counters	6	9	12	15	18	21	24	27

2.

Triangle	Difference in the number of counters used from the previous triangle	Pattern formed	Number of counters used
1	–	3 × 1 + 3	6
2	3	3 × 2 + 3	9
3	3	3 × 3 + 3	12
4	3	3 × 4 + 3	15
5	3	3 × 5 + 3	18
6	3	3 × 6 + 3	21
7	3	3 × 7 + 3	24
8	3	3 × 8 + 3	27

3. $3n + 3$

4. Triangle 175 = 3(175) + 3
   = 528 counters
   Triangle 200 = 3(200) + 3
   = 603 counters

5. Answers will vary. From the tables, students should notice that the pattern involves a multiple of the triangle number and a constant, that is, 3 counters.

Lesson 8.2 Activity (pp. 87–88)

Answers will vary.

Chapter 8 Project (p. 92)

Answers will vary. Sample:

Soup

Description of food	Food group	Quantity	Fat (grams)	Food energy (calories)
Vegetarian soup	Vegetable	0.5 cup	1	35

Main Dish

Description of food	Food group	Quantity	Fat (grams)	Food energy (calories)
Roasted lamb rib (lean)	Meat	1 oz	9	105
Broccoli (cooked)	Vegetable	0.5 cup	0	25
Corn (cooked, yellow)	Grain	1 ear	1	85

Dessert

Description of food	Food group	Quantity	Fat (grams)	Food energy (calories)
Carrot cake	Vegetable	1 piece	21	386
Banana	Fruit	1	1	114

Lesson 9.1 Activity (p. 105)

1–4. Answers will vary, based on students' strategies.

Chapter 9 Project (p. 110)

1. Answers will vary.

2. Answers vary, based on the data collected by the students.

3. Answers will vary, based on the data collected by the students. Students may choose to plot values for all rubber bands in one graph or separate them in different graphs.

4. Answers will vary. The data should approximate a linear pattern.

5. Answers will vary.

6. Answers will vary. The ratios $\frac{\text{adjusted length}}{\text{mass}}$ should be approximately equal.

7. Answers will vary.
If rubber bands are of different types, the longer stretch may be due to the composition of the material used to make the rubber bands, or due to the thickness of the rubber bands.

Lessons 10.1–10.3 Activity (p. 114)

Problem	Answer
Triangle, base = 8 m, height = 5 m, area = ?	20 m²
Triangle, area = 75 km², base = 5 km, height = ?	30 km
Triangle, area = 82.5 yd², height = 11 yd, base = ?	15 yd
Triangle, base = 12 cm, height = 10 cm, area = ?	60 cm²
Triangle, area = 25.5 ft², height = 3 ft, base = ?	17 ft
Triangle, area = 87 mi², base = 12 mi, height = ?	14.5 mi
Triangle, base = 4 yd, height = 12 yd, area = ?	24 yd²
Triangle, area = 29.75 in.², base = 7 in., height = ?	8.5 in.
Triangle, area = 40 m², height = 8 m, base = ?	10 m
Triangle, base = 7 cm, height = 7 cm, area = ?	24.5 cm²
Parallelogram, area = 136 m², height = 16 m, base = ?	8.5 m
Parallelogram, base = 4.5 km, height = 8 km, area = ?	36 km²
Parallelogram, area = 54 yd², base = 9 yd, height = ?	6 yd
Parallelogram, base = 14 m, height = 5.6 m, area = ?	78.4 m²

Problem	Answer
Parallelogram, height = 6 km, area = 105 km², base = ?	17.5 km
Trapezoid, base₁ = 3 cm, base₂ = 8 cm, height = 8 cm, area = ?	44 cm²
Trapezoid, base₁ = 12 yd, base₂ = 7 yd, height = 4 yd, area = ?	38 yd²
Trapezoid, base₁ = 12 m, base₂ = 16 m, height = 12 m, area = ?	168 m²
Trapezoid, base₁ = 12 cm, base₂ = 14 cm, height = 8 cm, area = ?	104 cm²
Trapezoid, base₁ = 10 yd, base₂ = 11 yd, height = 10 yd, area = ?	105 yd²
Trapezoid, base₁ = 16 mi, base₂ = 9 mi, height = 15 mi, area = ?	187.5 mi²
Pentagon, side length = 12 ft, height of a triangle = 8.26 ft, area = ?	247.8 ft²
Hexagon, side length = 5.2 in., height of a triangle = 4.5 in., area = ?	70.2 in.²
Hexagon, side length = 8 m, height of a triangle = 6.93 m, area = ?	166.32 m²

Chapter 10 Project (p. 122)

1. Answers will vary. Students can form a triangle or a square out of the four polygons, as shown below.
If they form a triangle, measure the base and the height to find the area.

If they form a square, measure the sides to find the area.

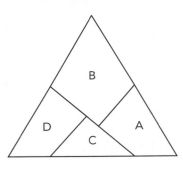

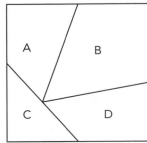

2. The total area of the four polygons is 196 cm².
   The length of one side of the square is 14 cm.

Lesson 11.2 Activity (p. 126)

1. Answers will vary. There is likely to be a slight difference in the two areas.

2. The following may cause the differences in measurements:
   - The way the diameter was measured. Some students may approximate the diameter as shown below (the dashed line is the actual diameter).

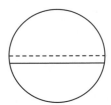

   - Measurement errors, brought about by the tools we use to measure (such as the string), the way we read measurements from the ruler, and the estimations that we make, such as the value of π.

3. Answers will vary.

4. Answers will vary.

Chapter 11 Project (p. 130)

1. Answers will vary. One angle in each triangle should be a right angle.

2. Answers will vary, but should include the conclusion that a triangle inscribed in a semicircle is a right triangle.

Lesson 12.3 Activity (p. 134)

1–3. Answers will vary. Answers are given based on a piece of paper that is 8 in. × 12 in.

1. Volume = length × width × height
   $$= 2 \times 2 \times 12$$
   $$= 48 \text{ in.}^3$$

2. Volume = length × width × height
   $$= 3 \times 3 \times 8$$
   $$= 72 \text{ in.}^3$$

3. Volume = Area of base × height
   $$= \frac{1}{2} \times 4 \times 3 \times 8$$
   $$= 48 \text{ in.}^3$$

4. Answers vary depending on the dimensions of the piece of paper used.

Chapter 12 Project (p. 138)

1. Answers will vary, depending on the piece of furniture used.
   For the given drawing of furniture: Find the total surface area inside and out, except for the bottom surface. This will give the amount of decorative paper required to wrap the furniture.

   Sides, back, top, and front:
   2(120 cm × 42 cm) + (120 cm × 40 cm) + (42 cm × 40 cm) + (5[2 cm × 36 cm] + 2[2 cm × 120 cm])
   = 10,080 cm² + 4,800 cm² + 1,680 cm² + 360 cm² + 480 cm²
   = 17,400 cm²

Inside:
8(36 cm × 40 cm) + 2(30 cm × 40 cm)
+ 4(20 cm × 40 cm) + 2(40 cm × 40 cm)
+ (30 cm × 36 cm) + 2(20 cm × 36 cm)
+ (36 cm × 40 cm)
= 11,520 cm² + 2,400 cm² + 3,200 cm²
   + 3,200 cm² + 1,080 cm² + 1,440 cm²
   + 1,440 cm²
= 24,280 cm²

Total surface area:
17,400 cm² + 24,280 cm² = 41,680 cm²

2. Answers will vary, depending on the piece of furniture used.
For the given drawing of furniture:
Find the dimensions of the inside of each layer of the cabinet.

1st layer from the top:
40 cm by 36 cm by 30 cm
2nd and 3rd layers:
40 cm by 36 cm by 20 cm
Bottom layer:
40 cm by 36 cm by 40 cm

Since the containers of the art materials measure 20 cm by 12 cm by 10 cm, you can fit 6 × 3 = 18 containers in the top layer, 6 × 2 = 12 containers each for the 2nd and 3rd layers, and 6 × 4 = 24 containers in the bottom layer.

Lesson 13.1 Activity (p. 142)

Answers will vary, based on the survey questions the students will write.

Chapter 13 Project (p. 146)

Answers will vary based on the statistical questions the students will write.

Lesson 14.1 Activity (p. 150)

1. Counting each digit will be easier if numbers are listed this way.

1	11	21	31	41	51	61	71	81	91
2	12	22	32	42	52	62	72	82	92
3	13	23	33	43	53	63	73	83	93
4	14	24	34	44	54	64	74	84	94
5	15	25	35	45	55	65	75	85	95
6	16	26	36	46	56	66	76	86	96
7	17	27	37	47	57	67	77	87	97
8	18	28	38	48	58	68	78	88	98
9	19	29	39	49	59	69	79	89	99
10	20	30	40	50	60	70	80	90	

2.

Digit	0	1	2	3	4	5	6	7	8	9
Frequency	9	20	20	20	20	20	20	20	20	20

3. Total frequency for the odd digits
(1, 3, 5, 7, and 9) = 100
The mean occurrence for the odd digits is
100 ÷ 5 = 20.

Total frequency for the even digits
(0, 2, 4, 6, and 8) = 89
The mean occurrence for the even digits is
89 ÷ 5 = 17.8.

Chapter 14 Project (p. 154)

1–4. Answers will vary, based on the data collected by the students.